Allyn and Bacon

Quick Guide to the Internet
for
Special Education

2000 Edition

Mary Male

San Jose State University

Doug Gotthoffer

California State University–Northridge

Allyn and Bacon

Boston • London • Toronto • Sydney • Tokyo • Singapore

Vice President and Director, Allyn and Bacon Interactive: Kevin B. Stone
Multimedia Editor: Marnie S. Greenhut
Editorial Production Administrator, Media: Robert Tonner
Cover Designer: Jennifer Hart
Editorial Production Service: Omegatype Typography, Inc.

NOTICE: Between the time web site information is gathered and then published it is not unusual for some sites to have closed. Also, the transcription of URLs can result in unintended typographical errors. The publisher would appreciate notification where these occcur so that they may be corrected in subsequent editions. Thank you.

TRADEMARK CREDITS: Where information was available, trademarks and registered trademarks are indicated below. When detailed information was not available, the publisher has indicated trademark status with an initial capital where those names appear in the text.

Macintosh is a registered trademark of Apple Computer, Inc.

Microsoft is a registered trademark of Microsoft Corporation. Windows, Windows95, and Microsoft Internet Explorer are trademarks of Microsoft Corporation.

Netscape and the Netscape Navigator logo are registered trademarks of Netscape Communications Corporation.

Copyright © 2000 by Allyn and Bacon
A Pearson Education Company
Needham Heights, Massachusetts 02494
Internet: www.abacon.com

ISBN 0-205-31054-0

Printed in the United States of America

10   9   8   7   6   5   4   3   2   1   02   01   00   99

Contents

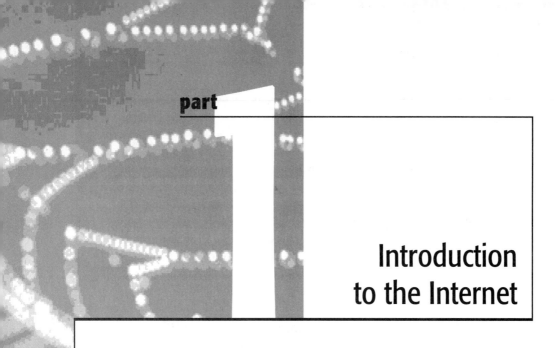

Introduction to the Internet

You're about to embark on an exciting experience as you become one of the millions of citizens of the Internet. In spite of what you might have heard, the Internet can be mastered by ordinary people before they earn a college degree and even if they're not majoring in rocket science.

Some Things You Ought to Know

Much of the confusion over the Internet comes from two sources. One is terminology. Just as the career you're preparing for has its own special vocabulary, so does the Internet. You'd be hard pressed to join in the shoptalk of archeologists, librarians, or carpenters if you didn't speak their language. Don't expect to plop yourself down in the middle of the Internet without some buzzwords under your belt, either.

The second source of confusion is that there are often many ways to accomplish the same ends on the Internet. This is a direct by-product of the freedom so highly cherished by Net citizens. When someone has an idea for doing something, he or she puts it out there and lets the Internet community decide its merits. As a result, it's difficult to put down in writing the *one exact* way to send email or find information on slugs or whatever.

In addition, there are differences in the workings of a PC or Mac and the various versions of the two major browsers, Netscape Communicator (or Navigator) and Internet Explorer. If you can't find a particular command or function mentioned in the book on your computer,

1

chances are it's there, but in a different place or with a slightly different name. Check the manual or online help that came with your computer, or ask a more computer-savvy friend or professor.

And relax. Getting up to speed on the Internet takes a little time, but the effort will be well rewarded. Approach learning your way around the Internet with the same enthusiasm and curiosity you approach learning your way around a new college campus. This isn't a competition. Nobody's keeping score. And the only winner will be you.

In *Understanding Media,* Marshall McLuhan presaged the existence of the Internet when he described electronic media as an extension of our central nervous system. On the other hand, today's students introduced to the Internet for the first time describe it as "Way cool."

No matter which description you favor, you are immersed in a period in our culture that is transforming the way we live by transforming the nature of the information we live by. As recently as 1980, intelligence was marked by "knowing things." If you were born in that year, by the time you were old enough to cross the street by yourself, that definition had changed radically. Today, in a revolution that makes McLuhan's vision tangible, events, facts, rumors, and gossip are distributed instantly to all parts of the global body. The effects are equivalent to a shot of electronic adrenaline. No longer the domain of the privileged few, information is shared by all the inhabitants of McLuhan's global village. Meanwhile, the concept of information as intelligence feels as archaic as a television remote control with a wire on it (ask your parents about that).

With hardly more effort than it takes to rub your eyes open in the morning you can connect with the latest news, with gossip about your favorite music group or TV star, with the best places to eat on spring break, with the weather back home, or with the trials and tribulations of that soap opera character whose life conflicts with your history class.

You can not only carry on a real-time conversation with your best friend at a college half a continent away you can see and hear her, too. Or, you can play interactive games with a dozen or more world-wide, world-class, challengers; and that's just for fun.

When it comes to your education, the Internet has shifted the focus from amassing information to putting that information to use. Newspaper and magazine archives are now almost instantly available, as are the contents of many reference books. Distant and seemingly unapproachable, experts are found answering questions in discussion groups or in electronic newsletters.

The Internet also addresses the major problem facing all of us in our split-second, efficiency-rated culture: Where do we find the time? The

Internet allows professors and students to keep in touch, to collaborate and learn, without placing unreasonable demands on individual schedules. Professors are posting everything from course syllabi to homework solutions on the Internet, and are increasingly answering questions online, all in an effort to ease the pressure for face-to-face meetings by supplementing them with cyberspace offices. The Internet enables students and professors to expand office hours into a twenty-four-hour-a-day, seven-day-a-week operation. Many classes have individual sites at which enrolled students can gather electronically to swap theories, ideas, resources, gripes, and triumphs.

By freeing us from some of the more mundane operations of information gathering, and by sharpening our information-gathering skills in other areas, the Internet encourages us to be more creative and imaginative. Instead of devoting most of our time to gathering information and precious little to analyzing and synthesizing it, the Internet tips the balance in favor of the skills that separate us from silicon chips. Other Internet citizens can gain the same advantage, however, and as much as the Internet ties us together, it simultaneously emphasizes our individual skills—our ability to connect information in new, meaningful, and exciting ways. Rarely have we had the opportunity to make connections and observations on such a wide range of topics, to create more individual belief systems, and to chart a path through learning that makes information personally useful and meaningful.

part

1

A Brief History of the Internet

The 20th century's greatest advance in personal communication and freedom of expression began as a tool for national defense. In the mid-1960s, the Department of Defense was searching for an information analogy to the new Interstate Highway System, a way to move computations and computing resources around the country in the event the Cold War caught fire. The immediate predicament, however, had to do with the Defense Department's budget, and the millions of dollars spent on computer research at universities and think tanks. Much of these millions was spent on acquiring, building, or modifying large computer systems to meet the demands of the emerging fields of computer graphics, artificial intelligence, and multiprocessing (where one computer was shared among dozens of different tasks).

While this research was distributed across the country, the unwieldy, often temperamental, computers were not. Though researchers at MIT had spare time on their computer, short of packing up their notes and traveling to Massachusetts, researchers at Berkeley had no way to use it. Instead, Berkeley computer scientists would wind up duplicating MIT hardware in California. Wary of being accused of re-inventing the wheel, the Advanced Research Projects Agency (ARPA), the funding arm of the Defense Department, invested in the ARPANET, a private network that would allow disparate computer systems to communicate with each other. Researchers could remain ensconced among their colleagues at their home campuses while using computing resources at government research sites thousands of miles away.

A small cadre of ARPANET citizens soon began writing computer programs to perform little tasks across the Internet. Most of these programs, while ostensibly meeting immediate research needs, were written for the challenge of writing them. These programmers, for example, created the first email systems. They also created games like Space Wars and Adventure. Driven in large part by the novelty and practicality of email, businesses and institutions accepting government research funds begged and borrowed their way onto the ARPANET, and the number of connections swelled.

As the innocence of the 1960s gave way the business sense of the 1980s, the government eased out of the networking business, turning the ARPANET (now Internet) over to its users. While we capitalize the word "Internet", it may surprise you to learn there is no "Internet, Inc.," no business in charge of this uniquely postmodern creation. Administration of this world-wide communication complex is still handled by the cooperating institutions and regional networks that comprise the Internet. The word "Internet" denotes a specific interconnected network of networks, and not a corporate entity.

part

1

Using the World Wide Web for Research

Just as no one owns the worldwide communication complex that is the Internet, there is no formal organization among the collection of hundreds of thousands of computers that make up the part of the Net called the World Wide Web.

If you've never seriously used the Web, you are about to take your first steps on what can only be described as an incredible journey. Initially, though, you might find it convenient to think of the Web as a giant television network with millions of channels. It's safe to say that, among all these channels, there's something for you to watch. Only, how to find it? You could click through the channels one by one, of course, but by the time you found something of interest it would (1) be over or (2) leave you wondering if there wasn't something better on that you're missing.

A more efficient way to search for what you want would be to consult some sort of TV listing. While you could skim through pages more rapidly than channels, the task would still be daunting. A more creative approach would allow you to press a button on your remote control that would connect you to a channel of interest; what's more, that channel would contain the names (or numbers) of other channels with similar programs. Those channels in turn would contain information about other channels. Now you could zip through this million-channel universe, touching down only at programs of potential interest. This seems far more effective than the hunt-and-peck method of the traditional couch potato.

If you have a feel for how this might work for television, you have a feel for what it's like to journey around (or surf) the Web. Instead of channels on the Web, we have *Web sites*. Each site contains one or more *pages*. Each page may contain, among other things, links to other pages, either in the same site or in other sites, anywhere in the world. These other pages may elaborate on the information you're looking at or may direct you to related but not identical information, or even provide contrasting or contradictory points of view; and, of course, these pages could have links of their own.

Web sites are maintained by businesses, institutions, affinity groups, professional organizations, government departments, and ordinary people anxious to express opinions, share information, sell products, or provide services. Because these Web sites are stored electronically, updating them is more convenient and practical than updating printed media. That makes Web sites far more dynamic than other types of research material you may be used to, and it means a visit to a Web site can open up new opportunities that weren't available as recently as a few hours ago.

part

1

Hypertext and Links

The invention that unveils these revolutionary possibilities is called *hypertext*. Hypertext is a technology for combining text, graphics, sounds, video, and links on a single World Wide Web page. Click on a link and you're transported, like Alice falling down the rabbit hole, to a new page, a new address, a new environment for research and communication.

Links come in three flavors: text, picture, and hot spot. A text link may be a letter, a word, a phrase, a sentence, or any contiguous combination of text characters. You can identify text links at a glance because

Text
Link

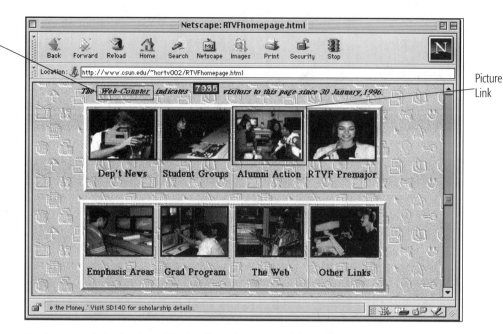

Picture
Link

Text links are underlined and set of in color. Picture links are set off by a colored border. Hot spots carry no visual identification.

the characters are <u>underlined</u>, and are often displayed in a unique color, setting the link apart from the rest of the text on the page. Picture links are pictures or other graphic elements. On the Web, a picture may not only be worth a thousand words, but it may also be the start of a journey into a whole new corner of cyberspace.

The third kind of link, the hot spot, is neither underlined nor bordered, a combination which would make it impossible to spot, were it not for a Web convention that offers you a helping hand finding all types of links. This helping hand is, well, a hand. Whenever the mouse cursor passes over a link, the cursor changes from an arrow to a hand. Wherever you see the hand icon, you can click and retrieve another Web page. Sweep the cursor over an area of interest, see the hand, follow the link, and you're surfing the Web.

In the Name of the Page

Zipping around the Web in this way may seem exciting, even serendipitous, but it's also fraught with perils. How, for instance, do you revisit a page of particular interest? Or share a page with a classmate? Or cite a page as a reference for a professor? Web page designers assign names, or titles, to their pages; unfortunately, there's nothing to prevent two designers from assigning the same title to different pages.

An instrument that uniquely identifies Web pages does exist. It's called a Universal Resource Locator (URL), the cyber-signposts of the World Wide Web. URLs contain all the information necessary to locate:

- the page containing the information you're looking for;
- the computer that hosts (stores) that page of information;
- the form the information is stored in.

A typical URL looks like this:

```
http://www.abacon.com/index.html
```

You enter it into the **Location** or **Address** field at the top of your browser window. Hit the **Return** (or **Enter**) key and your browser will deliver to your screen the exact page specified. When you click on a link, you're actually using a shorthand alternative to typing the URL yourself because the browser does it for you. In fact, if you watch the "Location" or "Address" field when you click on a link, you'll see its contents change to the URL you're traveling to.

part

1

The URL Exposed

How does your browser—or the whole World Wide Web structure, for that matter—know where you're going? As arcane as the URL appears, there is a logical explanation to its apparent madness. (This is true not only of URLs but also of your computer experience in general. Because a computer's "intelligence" only extends to following simple instructions exactly, most of the commands, instructions, and procedures you'll encounter have simple underlying patterns. Once you familiarize yourself with these patterns, you'll find you're able to make major leaps in your understanding of new Internet features.)

To unscramble the mysteries of World Wide Web addresses, we'll start at the end of the URL and work our way toward the front.

```
/index.html
```

This is the name of a single file or document. Eventually, the contents of this file/document will be transferred over the Internet to your computer.

However, because there are undoubtedly thousands of files on the Internet with this name, we need to clarify our intentions a bit more.

```
www.abacon.com
```

This is the name of a particular Internet *Web server,* a computer whose job it is to forward Web pages to you on request. By Internet convention, this name is unique. The combination of

```
www.abacon.com/index.html
```

identifies a unique file/document on a unique Web server on the World Wide Web. No other file has this combined address, so there's no question about which file/document to transfer to you.

The characters *http://* at the beginning of the URL identify the method by which the file/document will be transferred. The letters stand for HyperText Transfer Protocol.

Quick Check

Don't Be Lost In (Hyper)Space

Let's pause for a quick check of your Web navigation skills. Look at the sample web page on the next page. How many links does it contain?

Did you find all five? That's right, five:

■ The word "links" in the second line below the seaside picture;

■ The sentence "What about me?";

■ The word "cyberspace" in the quick brown fox sentence;

■ The red and white graphic in the lower left-hand corner of the page. The blue border around it matches the blue of the text links;

■ The hot spot in the seaside picture. We know there's at least one link in the picture, because the cursor appears as a hand. (There may be more hot spots on the page, but we can't tell from this picture alone.)

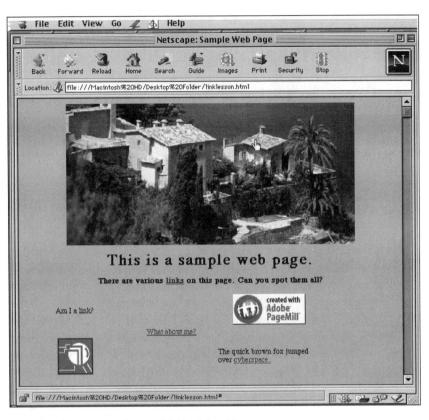

A sample web page to exercise your link identifying skills.

part

1

Getting There from Here

Now you know that a URL uniquely identifies a page and that links used as shorthand for URLs enable you to travel from page to page in the Web; but what if a link takes you someplace you don't want to go? Missing page messages take several forms, such as URL 404, Object not on this server, Missing Object, Page not Found, but they all lead to the same place—a dead end. The page specified by the link or URL no longer exists. There are many reasons for missing pages. You may have entered the URL incorrectly. Every character must be precise and no spaces are allowed. More than likely, though, especially if you arrived here via a link, the page you're after has been moved or removed. Remember, anybody can create a link to any page. In the spirit of the Internet, there are no forms to fill out, no procedures to follow. That's the good news. The bad news is that the owner of a page is under no

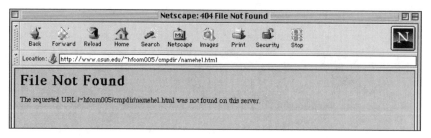

A missing page message, an all too common road hazard on the information superhighway.

obligation to inform the owners of links pointing to it that the page location has changed. In fact, there's no way for the page owner to even know about all the links to her page. Yes, the Internet's spirit of independence proves frustrating sometimes, but you'll find these small inconveniences are a cheap price to pay for the benefits you receive. Philosophy aside, though, we're still stuck on a page of no interest to us. The best strategy is to back up and try another approach.

part

1

Every time you click on the **Back** button, you return to the previous page you visited. That's because your browser keeps track of the pages you visit and the order in which you visit them. The **Back** icon, and its counterpart, the **Forward** icon, allow you to retrace the steps, forward and backward, of your cyberpath. Sometimes you may want to move two, three, or a dozen pages at once. Although you can click the **Back** or **Forward** icons multiple times, Web browsers offer an easier navigation shortcut. If you use Netscape, clicking on the **Go** menu in the menu bar displays a list of your most recently visited pages, in the order you've been there. Unlike the **Back** or **Forward** icons, you can select any page from the menu, and a single click takes you directly there. There's no need to laboriously move one page a time. If you use Internet Explorer, you can click on the **History** button in the Explorer bar to see a list of links you visited in previous days and weeks, or press the arrow at the end of the Address bar to see previously visited links.

Quick Check

As a quick review, here's what we know about navigating the Web so far:

- Enter a URL directly into the Location field;
- Click on a link;
- Use the **Back** or **Forward** icons;
- Select a page from the **Go** menu.

You Can Go Home (and to Other Pages) Again

How do we return to a page hours, days, or even months later? One way is to write down the URLs of every page we may want to revisit. There's got to be a better way, and there is: We call them bookmarks (on Netscape Communicator) or favorites (on Microsoft Internet Explorer).

Like their print book namesakes, Web bookmarks (and favorites) flag specific Web pages. Selecting an item from the **Bookmark/Favorites** menu, like selecting an item from the **Go** menu, is the equivalent of entering a URL into the **Location** field of your browser, except that items in the **Bookmark/Favorites** menu are ones you've added yourself and represent pages visited over many surfing experiences, not just the most recent one.

To select a page from your bookmark list, pull down the **Bookmark/Favorites** menu and click on the desired entry. In Netscape Communicator, clicking on the **Add Bookmark** command makes a bookmark entry for the current page. **Add to Favorites** performs the same function in Microsoft Internet Explorer.

To save a favorite page location, use the **Add** feature available on both browsers. Clicking that feature adds the location of the current page to your **Bookmark/Favorites** menu. A cautionary note is in order here. Your bookmark or favorites list physically exists only on your personal computer, which means that if you connect to the Internet on a different computer, your list won't be available. If you routinely connect to the Internet from a computer lab, for example, get ready to carry the URLs for your favorite Web sites in your notebook or your head.

part

1

Searching and Search Engines

Returning to our cable television analogy, you may recall that we conveniently glossed over the question of how we selected a starting channel in the first place. With a million TV channels, or several million Web pages, we can't depend solely on luck guiding us to something interesting.

On the Web, we solve the problem with specialized computer programs called *search engines* that crawl through the Web, page by page, cataloging its contents. As different software designers developed search strategies, entrepreneurs established Web sites where any user could find pages containing particular words and phrases. Today, Web sites such as Yahoo!, AltaVista, Excite, WebCrawler, and MetaCrawler offer you a "front door" to the Internet that begins with a search for content of interest.

The URLs for some popular search sites are:

Excite	`www.excite.com`
Yahoo!	`www.yahoo.com`
AltaVista	`www.altavista.digital.com`
WebCrawler	`www.webcrawler.com`
MetaCrawler	`www.metacrawler.com`
Infoseek	`www.infoseek.com`
EBlast	`www.eblast.com`
HotBot	`www.hotbot.com`

Internet Gold Is Where You Find It

part 1

Let's perform a simple search using HotBot to find information about the history of the Internet.

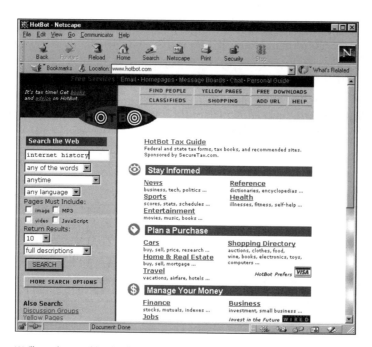

We'll start by searching for the words "internet" or "history." By looking for "any of the words," the search will return pages on which either "internet" or "history" or both appear.

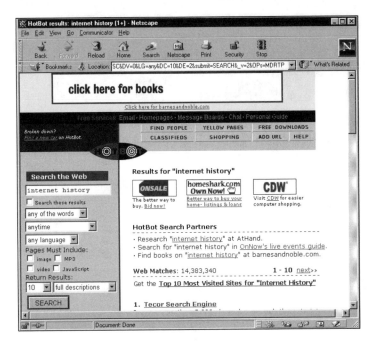

Our search returned 14,383,340 matches or *hits*. Note that the first item doesn't seem to be Internet history–related. By viewing the percentage number in the last line of each summary, you will be able to see the "quality" of the match, which is usually related to the number of times the search word(s) appears on the page.

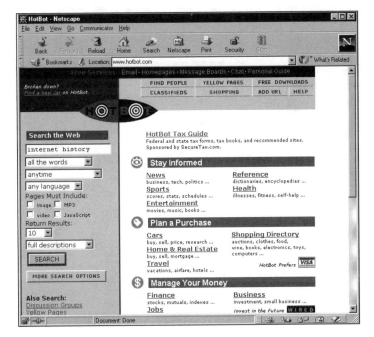

We can conduct the same search, but this time look for "all the words." The search will return hits when both "internet" and "history" appear on the same page, in any order, and not necessarily next to each other.

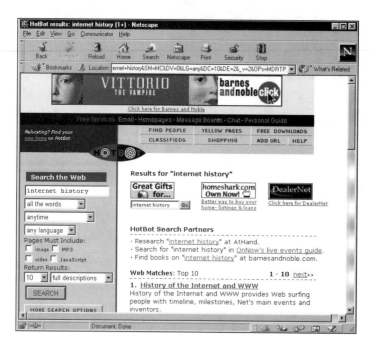

The search is narrowed down somewhat, but it is still not providing us with the information we need.

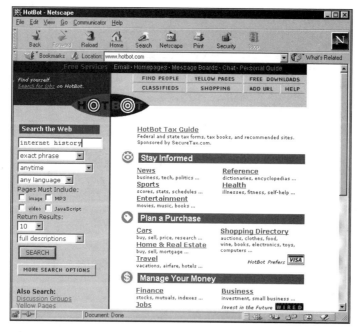

When we search for the exact phrase "internet history," which means those two words in exactly that order, with no intervening words, we're down to about 6,000 hits (still a substantial number).

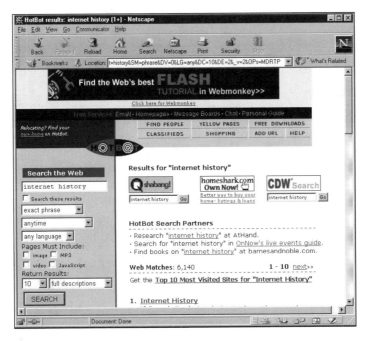

As you can see, the first hit seems to be more specific. However, other hits in the list may have nothing to do with the history of the Internet. Hits happen. No search engine is 100 percent accurate 100 percent of the time. Spurious search results are the serendipity of the Internet. Look at them as an opportunity to explore something new.

Out of curiosity, let's try our history of the Internet search using a different search engine. When we search for the phrase "history of the internet" using WebCrawler, the quotation marks serve the same purpose as selecting "the exact phrase" option in Hotbot. The WebCrawler search only finds 504 hits. Some are the same as those found using HotBot, some are different. Different searching strategies and software algorithms make using more than one search engine a must for serious researchers.

The major search engines conveniently provide you with tips to help you get the most out of their searches. These include ways to use AND and OR to narrow down searches, and ways to use NOT to eliminate unwanted hits.

Each search engine also uses a slightly different approach to cataloging the Web, so at different sites your results might vary. Often, one search engine provides better results (more relevant hits) in your areas of interest; sometimes, the wise strategy is to provide the same input to several different engines. No one search engine does a perfect job all the time, so experience will dictate the one that's most valuable for you.

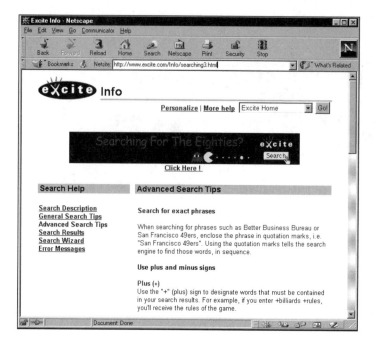

You'll find search tip pages like this at all the major search engine sites.

Quick Check

Let's review our searching strategies:

- Visit one of the search engine sites;
- Enter key words or phrases that best describe the search criteria;
- Narrow the search if necessary by using options such as "all the words" or "the exact phrase." On some search engines, you may use the word "and" or the symbol "|" to indicate words that all must appear on a page;
- Try using the same criteria with different search engines.

How Not to Come Down with a Virus

Downloading files from the Internet allows less responsible Net citizens to unleash onto your computer viruses, worms, and Trojan horses, all dangerous programs that fool you into thinking they're doing one thing while they're actually erasing your hard disk or performing some other undesirable task. Protection is your responsibility.

One way to reduce the risk of contracting a virus is to download software from reliable sites. Corporations such as Microsoft and Apple take care to make sure downloadable software is virus free. So do most institutions that provide software downloads as a public service (such as the Stanford University archives of Macintosh software). Be especially careful of programs you find on someone's home page. If you're not sure about safe download sources, ask around in a newsgroup (discussed shortly), talk to friends, or check with the information technology center on campus.

You can also buy and use a reliable virus program. Norton, Symantec, and Dr. Solomon all sell first-rate programs for the Mac and PC. You can update these programs right from the Internet so they'll detect the most current viruses. Most of the time, these programs can disinfect files/documents on your disk that contain viruses. Crude as it may sound, downloading programs from the Internet without using a virus check is like having unprotected sex with a stranger. While downloading software may not be life threatening, imagine the consequences if your entire hard disk, including all your course work and software, is totally obliterated. It won't leave you feeling very good.

part

1

If you'd like some entertaining practice sharpening your Web searching skills, point your browser to <www.internettreasurehunt.com>, follow the directions, and you're on your way to becoming an Internet researcher extraordinaire.

The (E)mail Goes Through

Email was one of the first applications created for the Internet by its de-signers, who sought a method of communicating with each other directly from their keyboards. Your electronic Internet mailbox is to email what a post office box is to "snail mail" (the name Net citizens apply to ordi-nary, hand-delivered mail). This mailbox resides on the computer of your Internet Service Provider (ISP). That's the organization providing you with your Internet account. Most of the time your ISP will be your school; but, you may contract with one of the commercial providers, such as America Online, Netcom, Microsoft Network, Earthlink, or AT&T. The Internet doesn't deliver a message to your door but instead leaves it in a conveniently accessible place (your mailbox) in the post of-fice (the computer of your ISP), until you retrieve the mail using your combination (password).

If you currently have computer access to the Internet, your school or ISP assigned you a *user name* (also called a user id, account name, or account number). This user name may be your first name, your first initial and the first few characters of your last name, or some strange combination of numbers and letters only a computer could love. An email address is a combination of your user name and the unique ad-dress of the computer through which you access your email, like this:

```
username@computername.edu
```

The three letters after the dot, in this case "edu," identify the top level "domain." There are six common domain categories in use: edu (edu-cational), com (commercial), org (organization), net (network), mil (mili-tary), and gov (government). The symbol "@"—called the "at" sign in typewriter days—serves two purposes: For computers, it provides a neat, clean separation between your user name and the computer name; for people, it makes Internet addresses more pronounceable. Your address is read: user name "at" computer name "dot" e-d-u. Suppose your Internet user name is "a4736g" and your ISP is Allyn & Bacon, the publisher of this book. Your email address might look like

```
a4736g@abacon.com
```

and you would tell people your email address is "ay-four-seven-three-six-gee at ay bacon dot com."

We Don't Just Handle Your Email, We're Also a Client

You use email with the aid of special programs called *mail clients*. As with search engines, mail clients have the same set of core features, but your access to these features varies with the type of program. On both the PC and the Mac, Netscape Communicator and Microsoft Internet Explorer give you access to mail clients while you're plugged into the Web. That way you can pick up and send mail while you're surfing the Web.

The basic email service functions are creating and sending mail, reading mail, replying to mail, and forwarding mail. First we'll examine the process of sending and reading mail, and then we'll discuss how to set up your programs so that your messages arrive safely.

Let's look at a typical mail client screen, in this case from Netscape Communicator 4.5. You reach this screen by choosing **Messenger** from under the **Communicator** menu. To send a message from scratch, choose the **New Msg** button to create a blank message form, which has fields for the recipient's address and the subject, and a window for the text of the message.

Fill in the recipient's address in the "To" field, just above the arrow. Use your own address. We'll send email to ourselves and use the same

part

1

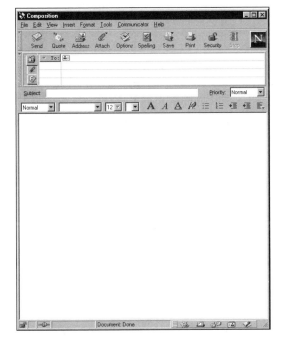

New message form, with fields for recipient's address and the subject, and a window for the text of the message.

message to practice sending email and reading it as well; then we'll know if your messages come out as expected.

Click in the "Subject" field and enter a word or phrase that generally describes the topic of the message. Since we're doing this for the first time, let's type "Maiden Email Voyage."

Now click anywhere in the text window and enter your message. Let's say "Hi. Thanks for guiding me through sending my first email." You'll find that the mail client works here like a word processing program, which means you can insert and delete words and characters and highlight text.

Now click the **Send** button on the Navigation toolbar. You've just created and sent your first email message. In most systems, it takes a few seconds to a few minutes for a message to yourself to reach your mailbox, so you might want to take a short break before continuing. When you're ready to proceed, close the **Composition** window and click the **Get Msg** button.

part

1

What Goes Around Comes Around

Now let's grab hold of the message you just sent to yourself. When retrieving mail, most mail clients display a window showing the messages in your mailbox telling you how many new messages have been added.

If you've never used your email before, chances are your message window is empty, or contains only one or two messages (usually official messages from the ISP) besides the one you sent to yourself. The message to yourself should be accompanied by an indicator of some sort—a colored mark, the letter N—indicating it's a new message. In Netscape Communicator, as in other mail clients, you also get to see the date of the message, who sent it, and the information you entered in the subject line. The Subject field lets you scan your messages and determine which ones you want to look at first.

The summary of received messages tells you everything you need to know about a message except what's in it. Click anywhere in the line to see the contents in the message window. Click on the message from yourself and you'll see the contents of the message displayed in a window. The information at the top—To, From, Subject, and so forth—is called the *header*. Depending on your system, you may also see some cryptic lines with terms such as X-Mailer, received by, and id number. Most of the time, there's nothing in this part of the header of interest, so just skip over it for now.

Moving Forward

The contents, or text, of your message can be cut and pasted just like any other text document. If you and a classmate are working on a project together, your partner can write part of a paper and email it to you, and you can copy the text from your email message and paste it into your word processing program.

What if there are three partners in this project? One partner sends you a draft of the paper for you to review. You like it and want to send it on to your other partner. The **Forward** feature lets you send the message intact, so you don't have to cut and paste it into a new message window. To forward a message, highlight it in the **Inbox** (top) and click the **Forward** icon. Enter the recipient's address in the "To" field of the message window. Note that the subject of the message is "Fwd:" followed by the subject of the original message. Use the text window to add your comments ahead of the original message.

A Chance to Reply

part
1

Email is not a one-way message system. Let's walk through a reply to a message from a correspondent named Elliot. Highlight the message in your **Inbox** again and this time click on the **Reply** icon. When the message window appears, click on the **Quote** icon. Depending on which program you're using, you'll see that each line in the message is preceded by either a vertical bar or a right angle bracket (>).

Note the vertical line to the left of the original text. The "To" and "Subject" fields are filled in automatically with the address of the sender and the original subject preceded by "Re:". In Internet terminology, the message has been *quoted*. The vertical bar or > is used to indicate lines not written by you but by someone else (in this case, the message's original author). Why bother? Because this feature allows you to reply without retyping the parts of the message you're responding to. Because your typing isn't quoted, your answers stand out from the original message. Netscape Communicator 4.5 adds some blank lines above and below your comments, a good practice for you if your mail client doesn't do this automatically.

Welcome to the Internet, Miss Manners

While we're on the subject of email, here are some *netiquette* (net etiquette) tips.

- When you send email to someone, even someone who knows you well, all they have to look at are your words—there's no body language attached. That means there's no smile, no twinkle in the eye, no raised eyebrow; and especially, there's no tone of voice. What you write is open to interpretation and your recipient has nothing to guide him or her. You may understand the context of a remark, but will your reader? If you have any doubts about how your message will be interpreted, you might want to tack on an *emoticon* to your message. An emoticon is a face created out of keyboard characters. For example, there's the happy Smiley :-) (you have to look at it sideways . . . the parenthesis is its mouth), the frowning Smiley :-((Frownie?), the winking Smiley ;-), and so forth. Smileys are the body language of the Internet. Use them to put remarks in context. "Great," in response to a friend's suggestion means you like the idea. "Great :-(" changes the meaning to one of disappointment or sarcasm. (Want a complete list of emoticons? Try using "emoticon" as a key word for a Web search.)

part

1

- Keep email messages on target. One of the benefits of email is its speed. Reading through lengthy messages leaves the reader wondering when you'll get to the point.

- Email's speed carries with it a certain responsibility. Its ease of use and the way a messages seems to cry out for an answer both encourage quick responses, but quick doesn't necessarily mean thoughtful. Once you hit the **Send** icon, that message is gone. There's no recall button. Think before you write, lest you feel the wrath of the modern-day version of your parents' adage: Answer in haste, repent at leisure.

Keeping Things to Yourself

Here's another tip cum cautionary note, this one about Web security. Just as you take care to protect your wallet or purse while walking down a crowded street, it's only good practice to exercise caution with information you'd like to keep (relatively) private. Information you pass around the Internet is stored on, or passed along by, computers that are accessible to others. Although computer system administrators take great care to insure the security of this information, no scheme is completely infallible. Here are some security tips:

- Exercise care when sending sensitive information such as credit card numbers, passwords, even telephone numbers and addresses in plain email. Your email message may pass through four or five computers en route to its destination, and at any of these points, it can be intercepted and read by someone other than the recipient.

- Send personal information over the Web only if the page is secure. Web browsers automatically encrypt information on secure pages, and the information can only be unscrambled at the Web site that created the secure page. You can tell if a page is secure by checking the status bar at the bottom of your browser's window for an icon of a closed lock.

- Remember that any files you store on your ISP's computer are accessible to unscrupulous hackers.

- Protect your password. Many Web client programs, such as mail clients, have your password for you. That means anyone with physical access to your computer can read your email. With a few simple tools, someone can even steal your password. Never leave your password on a lab computer. (Make sure the **Remember Password** or **Save Password** box is unchecked in any application that asks for your password.)

part

1

The closed lock icon in the lower left-hand corner of your browser window indicates a "secure" Web page.

An Audience Far Wider Than You Imagine

Remember that the Web in particular and the Internet in general are communications mediums with a far-reaching audience, and placing information on the Internet is tantamount to publishing it. Certainly, the contents of any message or page you post become public information, but in a newsgroup (an electronic bulletin board), your email address also becomes public knowledge. On a Web page, posting a photo of your favorite music group can violate the photographer's copyright, just as if you published the image in a magazine. Use common sense about posting information you or someone else expects to remain private; and, remember, information on the Web can and will be read by people with different tastes and sensitivities. The Web tends to be self-censoring, so be prepared to handle feedback, both good and bad.

A Discussion of Lists

There's no reason you can't use email to create a discussion group. You pose a question, for example, by sending an email message to everyone in the group. Somebody answers and sends the answer to everyone else on the list, and so on.

At least, that's the theory.

In practice, this is what often happens. As people join and leave the group, you and the rest of your group are consumed with updating your lists, adding new names and deleting old ones. As new people join, their addresses may not make it onto the lists of all the members of the group, so different participants get different messages. The work of administering the lists becomes worse than any value anyone can get out of the group, and so it quickly dissolves.

Generally, you're better off letting the computer handle discussion group administration. A *list server* is a program for administering emailing lists. It automatically adds and deletes list members and handles the distribution of messages.

part

1

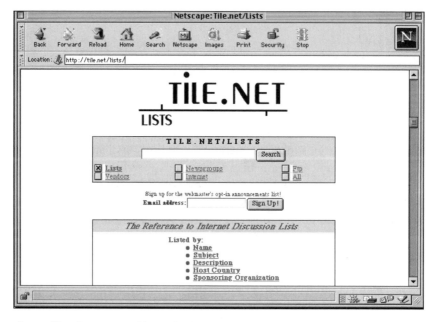

Tile.Net offfers shortcuts to working your way through the Internet's maze of discussion lists.

Thousands of mailing lists have already been formed by users with common interests. You may find mailing lists for celebrities, organizations, political interests, occupations, and hobbies. Your instructor may establish a mailing list for your course.

Groups come in several different flavors. Some are extremely active. You can receive as many as forty or more email messages a day. Other lists may send you a message a month. One-way lists, such as printed newsletters, do not distribute your reply to any other subscriber. Some lists distribute replies to everyone. These lists include mediated lists, in which an "editor" reviews each reply for suitability (relevance, tone, use of language) before distributing the message, and unmediated lists, in which each subscriber's response is automatically distributed to all the other subscribers with no restrictions except those dictated by decency and common sense, though these qualities may not always be obvious from reading the messages.

Get on a List Online

You join in the discussion by subscribing to a list, which is as straight-forward as sending email. You need to know only two items: the name of the list and the address of the list server program handling subscriptions. To join a list, send a **Subscribe** message to the list server address. The message must contain the letters "Sub," the name of the list, and your name (your real name, not your user name), all on one line. *And that's all.* This message will be read by a computer program that looks for these items only. At the very best, other comments in the message will be ignored. At the very worst, your entire message will be ignored, and so will you.

Within a few hours to a day after subscribing, the list server will automatically send you a confirmation email message, including instructions for sending messages, finding out information about the list and its members, and canceling your subscription. Save this message for future reference. That way, if you do decide to leave the list, you won't have to circulate a message to the members asking how to unsubscribe, and you won't have to wade through fifty replies all relaying the same information you received when you joined.

Soon after your confirmation message appears in your mailbox, and depending on the activity level of the list, you'll begin receiving email messages. New list subscribers customarily wait a while before joining the discussion. After all, you're electronically strolling into a room full of strangers; it's only fair to see what topics are being discussed before

part

1

wading in with your own opinions. Otherwise, you're like the bore at the party who elbows his way into a conversation with "But enough about you, let's talk about me." You'll also want to avoid the faux pas of posting a long missive on a topic that subscribers spent the preceding three weeks thrashing out. Observe the list for a while, understand its tone and feel, what topics are of interest to others and what areas are taboo. Also, look for personalities. Who's the most vociferous? Who writes very little but responds thoughtfully? Who's the most flexible? The most rigid? Most of all, keep in mind that there are far more observers than participants. What you write may be read by 10 or 100 times more people than those whose names show up in the daily messages.

When you reply to a message, you reply to the list server address, not to the address of the sender (unless you intend for your communication to remain private). The list server program takes care of distributing your message listwide. Use the address in the "Reply To" field of the message. Most mail clients automatically use this address when you select the **Reply** command. Some may ask if you want to use the reply address (say yes). Some lists will send a copy of your reply to you so you know your message is online. Others don't send the author a copy, relying on your faith in the infallibility of computers.

In the words of those famous late night television commercials, you can cancel your subscription at any time. Simply send a message to the address you used to subscribe (which you'll find on that confirmation message you saved for reference), with "Unsub," followed on the same line by the name of the list. For example, to leave a list named "WRITER-L," you would send:

```
Unsub WRITER-L
```

Even if you receive messages for a short while afterwards, have faith—they will disappear.

Waste Not, Want Not

List servers create an excellent forum for people with common interests to share their views; however, from the Internet standpoint, these lists are terribly wasteful. First of all, if there are one thousand subscribers to a list, every message must be copied one thousand times and distributed over the Internet. If there are forty replies a day, this one list creates forty thousand email messages. Ten such lists mean almost a half million messages, most of which are identical, flying around the Net.

part

1

Another wasteful aspect of list servers is the way in which messages are answered. The messages in your mailbox on any given day represent a combination of new topics and responses to previous messages. But where are these previous messages? If you saved them, they're in your email mailbox taking up disk space. If you haven't saved them, you have nothing to compare the response to. What if a particular message touches off a chain of responses, with subscribers referring not only to the source message but to responses as well? It sounds like the only safe strategy is to save every message from the list, a suggestion as absurd as it is impractical.

What we really need is something closer to a bulletin board than a mailing list. On a bulletin board, messages are posted once. Similar notices wind up clustered together. Everyone comes to the same place to read or post messages.

And Now the News(group)

The Internet equivalent of the bulletin board is the Usenet or newsgroup area. Usenet messages are copied only once for each ISP supporting the newsgroup. If there are one thousand students on your campus reading the same newsgroup message, there need only be one copy of the message stored on your school's computer.

Categorizing a World of Information

Newsgroups are categorized by topics, with topics broken down into subtopics and sub-subtopics. For example, you'll find newsgroups devoted to computers, hobbies, science, social issues, and "alternatives." Newsgroups in this last category cover a wide range of topics that may not appeal to the mainstream. Also in this category are beginning newsgroups.

Usenet names are amalgams of their topics and subtopics, separated by dots. If you were interested in a newsgroup dealing with, say, music, you might start with rec.music and move down to rec.music.radiohead, or rec.music.techno, and so forth. The naming scheme allows you to zero in on a topic of interest.

Getting into the News(group) Business

Most of the work of reading, responding to, and posting messages is handled by a news reader client program, accessible through both Netscape Communicator and Microsoft Internet Explorer. You can not only surf the Web and handle your mail via your browser, but you can also drop into your favorite newsgroups virtually all in one operation.

Let's drop into a newsgroup. To reach groups via Netscape Communicator 4.5, go to the Communicator menu bar and select **Newsgroups.** Then, from the File menu, select **Subscribe.** A dialogue box will open that displays a list of available groups.

To subscribe to a newsgroup—that is, to tell your news reader you want to be kept up-to-date on the messages posted to a particular group—highlight the group of interest and click on **Subscribe.** Alternately, you can click in the Subscribe column to the right of the group name. The check mark in the Subscribe column means you're "in."Now, click **OK.**

The message center in Netscape Communicator displays a list of newsgroups on your subscription list. Double click on the one of current interest and your reader presents you with a list of messages posted on the group's bulletin board. Double click on a message to open its contents in a window.

Often, messages contain "Re:" in their subject lines, indicating a response to a previous message (the letters stand for "Regarding"). Many news readers maintain a *thread* for you. Threads are chains of messages and all responses to that message. These readers give you the option to read messages chronologically or to read a message followed by its responses.

When you subscribe to a newsgroup, your news reader will also keep track of the messages you've read so that it can present you with the newest (unread) ones. While older messages are still available to you, this feature guarantees that you stay up-to-date without any record keeping on your part. Subscribing to a newsgroup is free, and the subscription information resides on your computer.

Newsgroups have no way of knowing who their subscribers are, and the same caveat that applies to bookmarks applies to newsgroups. Information about your subscriptions resides physically on the personal computer you're using. If you switch computers, as in a lab, your subscription information and history of read messages are beyond your reach.

part
1

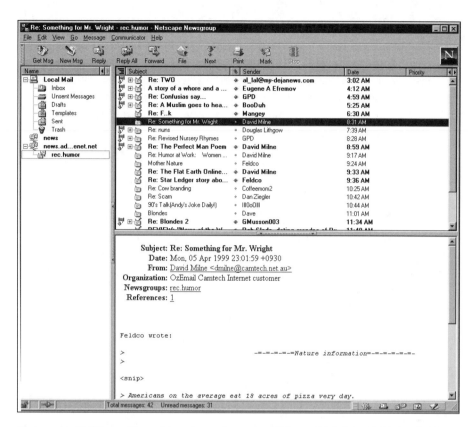

part

1

The top part of this figure shows a listing of posted messages. While not visible from this black and white reproduction, a red indicator in the Subject column marks unread messages. Double-clicking on a message opens its contents into a window shown in the bottom part of this figure. You can reply to this message via the Reply icon, or get the next message using the Next icon.

Welcome to the Internet, Miss Manners—Again

As with list servers, hang out for a while, or *lurk*, to familiarize yourself with the style, tone, and content of newsgroup messages. As you probably surmised from the names of the groups, their topics of discussion are quite narrow. One of the no-nos of newsgroups is posting messages on subjects outside the focus of the group. Posting off-topic messages, especially lengthy ones, is an excellent way to attract a flaming.

A *flame* is a brutally debasing message from one user to another. Flames are designed to hurt and offend, and often the target of the flame feels compelled to respond in kind to protect his or her self-esteem. This leads to a *flame war,* as other users take sides and wade in with flames of their own. If you find yourself the target of a flame, your best strategy is to ignore it. As with a campfire, if no one tends to the flames, they soon die out.

As mentioned earlier, posting messages to newsgroups is a modern form of publishing, and a publisher assumes certain responsibilities. You have a duty to keep your messages short and to the point. Many newsgroup visitors connect to the Internet via modems. Downloading a day's worth of long postings, especially uninteresting ones, is annoying and frustrating. Similarly, don't post the same message to multiple, re-lated newsgroups. This is called *cross posting,* and it's a peeve of Net citizens who check into these groups. If you've ever flipped the television from channel to channel during a commercial break only to encounter the same commercial (an advertising practice called *roadblocking*), you can imagine how annoying it is to drop in on several newsgroups only to find the same messages posted to each one.

With the huge potential audience newsgroups offer, you might think you've found an excellent medium for advertising goods or services. After all, posting a few messages appears analogous to running classified ads in newspapers, only here the cost is free. There's a name for these kinds of messages—*spam.* Spam is the junk mail of the Internet, and the practice of spamming is a surefire way to attract flames. The best advice for handling spam? Don't answer it. Not only does an answer encourage the spammer, but he or she will also undoubtedly put your email address on a list and sell it to other spammers, who will flood your online mail-box with their junk.

Above all, be considerate of others. Treat them the way you'd like to be treated. Do you enjoy having your grammar or word choices cor-rected in front of the whole world? Do you feel comfortable when some-one calls you stupid in public? Do you appreciate having your religion, ethnicity, heritage, or gender belittled in front of an audience? Respect the rights and feelings of others, if not out of simple decency then out of the sanctions your ISP may impose. Although you have every right to ex-press an unpopular opinion or to take issue with the postings of others, most ISPs have regulations about the kinds of messages one can send via their facilities. Obscenities, threats, and spam may, at a minimum, result in your losing your Internet access privileges.

part

1

Give Your Web Browser Some Personality—Yours

Before accessing email and newsgroup functions, you need to set up or personalize your browser. If you always work on the same personal computer, this is a one-time operation that takes only a few minutes. In it, you tell your browser where to find essential computer servers, along with personal information the Internet needs to move messages for you.

- *Step 1:*   Open the **Preferences** menu in Netscape or the **Internet Options** in Internet Explorer. In Netscape Communicator the Preferences menu is located under the **Edit** menu; in Microsoft Internet Explorer the Internet Options can be found under the **View** menu.

- *Step 2:*   Tell the browser who you are and where to find your mail servers. Your Reply To address is typically the same as your email address, though if you have an email alias you can use it here. Microsoft Internet Explorer has slots for your mail servers in the same window. Your ISP will provide the server names and addresses. Be sure to use your user name (and not your alias) in the "Account Name" field. SMTP handles your outgoing messages, while the POP3 server routes incoming mail. Often, but not always, these server names are the same. Netscape Communicator has a separate window for server names.

part

1

- *Step 3:*   Tell the browser where to find your news server. Your ISP will furnish the name of the server. Note that in Microsoft Internet Explorer, you specify a helper application to read the news. Now that most computers come with browsers already loaded onto the hard disk, you'll find that these helper applications are already set up for you.

- *Step 4:*   Set your home page. For convenience, you may want your browser to start by fetching a particular page, such as your favorite search site. Or you might want to begin at your school library's home page. Enter the URL for this starting page in the home page address field. Both Netscape and Microsoft offer the option of no home page when you start up. In that case, you get a blank browser window.

Operating systems such as Mac OS 8 and Microsoft Windows 95 offer automated help in setting up your browsers for Web, mail, and newsgroup operation. You need to know the names of the servers mentioned above, along with your user name and other details, such as the address of the domain name server (DNS) of your ISP. You should receive all this information when you open your Internet account. If not, ask for it.

Critical Evaluation

Where Seeing Is Not Always Believing

Typical research resources, such as journal articles, books, and other scholarly works, are reviewed by a panel of experts before being published. At the very least, any reputable publisher takes care to assure that the author is who he or she claims to be and that the work being published represents a reasoned and informed point of view. When anyone can post anything in a Web site or to a newsgroup, the burden of assessing the relevance and accuracy of what you read falls to you. Rumors quickly grow into facts on the Internet simply because stories can spread so rapidly that the "news" seems to be everywhere. Because the Internet leaves few tracks, in no time it's impossible to tell whether you are reading independent stories or the merely same story that's been around the world two or three times. Gathering information on the Internet may be quick, but verifying the quality of information requires a serious commitment.

Approach researching via the Internet with confidence, however, and not with trepidation. You'll find it an excellent workout for your critical evaluation skills; no matter what career you pursue, employers value an employee who can think critically and independently. Critical thinking is also the basis of problem solving, another ability highly valued by the business community. So, as you research your academic projects, be assured that you're simultaneously developing lifelong expertise.

It's Okay to Be Critical of Others

The first tip for successful researching on the Internet is to always consider your source. A Web site's URL often alerts you to the sponsor of the site. CNN or MSNBC are established news organizations, and you can give the information you find at their sites the same weight you would give to their cablecasts. Likewise, major newspapers operate Web sites with articles reprinted from their daily editions or expanded stories written expressly for the Internet. On the other hand, if you're unfamiliar with the source, treat the information the way you would any new data. Look for specifics—"66 percent of all voters" as opposed to "most voters"—and for information that can be verified—a cited report in another medium or information accessible through a Web site hosted by a credible sponsor—as opposed to generalities or unverifiable claims. Look for independent paths to the same information. This can involve careful use of search engines or visits to newsgroups with both similar and opposing viewpoints. Make sure that the "independent" information you find is truly independent. In newsgroups don't discount the possibility of multiple postings, or that a posting in one group is nothing more than a quotation from a posting in another. Ways to verify independent paths include following sources (if any) back to their origins, contacting the person posting a message and asking for clarification, or checking other media for verification.

In many cases, you can use your intuition and common sense to raise your comfort level about the soundness of the information. With both list servers and newsgroups, it's possible to lurk for a while to develop a feeling for the authors of various postings. Who seems the most authoritarian, and who seems to be "speaking" from emotion or bias? Who seems to know what he or she is talking about on a regular basis? Do these people cite their sources of information (a job or affiliation perhaps)? Do they have a history of thoughtful, insightful postings, or do their postings typically contain generalities, unjustifiable claims, or flames? On Web sites, where the information feels more anonymous, there are also clues you can use to test for authenticity. Verify who's hosting the Web site. If the host or domain name is unfamiliar to you, perhaps a search engine can help you locate more information. Measure the tone and style of the writing at the site. Does it seem consistent with the education level and knowledge base necessary to write intelligently about the subject?

part

1

When offering an unorthodox point of view, good authors supply facts, figures, and quotes to buttress their positions, expecting readers to be skeptical of their claims. Knowledgeable authors on the Internet follow these same commonsense guidelines. Be suspicious of authors who expect you to agree with their points of view simply because they've published them on the Internet. In one-on-one encounters, you frequently judge the authority and knowledge of the speaker using criteria you'd be hard pressed to explain. Use your sense of intuition on the Internet, too.

As a researcher (and as a human being), the job of critical thinking requires a combination of healthy skepticism and rabid curiosity. Newsgroups and Web sites tend to focus narrowly on single issues (newsgroups more so than Web sites). Don't expect to find a torrent of opposing views on newsgroup postings; their very nature and reason for existence dampens free-ranging discussions. A newsgroup on *The X-Files* might argue about whether extraterrestrials exist but not whether the program is the premier television show on the air today. Such a discussion would run counter to the purposes of the newsgroup and would be a violation of netiquette. Anyone posting such a message would be flamed, embarrassed, ignored, or otherwise driven away. Your research responsibilities include searching for opposing views by visiting a variety of newsgroups and Web sites. A help here is to fall back on the familiar questions of journalism: who, what, when, where, and why.

- **Who** else might speak knowledgeably on this subject? Enter that person's name into a search engine. You might be surprised to find whose work is represented on the Web. (For fun, one of the authors entered the name of a rock-and-roll New York radio disk jockey into MetaCrawler and was amazed to find several pages devoted to the DJ, including sound clips of broadcasts dating back to the sixties, along with a history of his theme song.)

- **What** event might shed more information on your topic? Is there a group or organization that represents your topic? Do they hold an annual conference? Are synopses of presentations posted on the sponsoring organization's Web site?

- **When** do events happen? Annual meetings or seasonal occurrences can help you isolate newsgroup postings of interest.

- **Where** might you find this information? If you're searching for information on wines, for example, check to see if major wine-producing regions, such as the Napa Valley in California or the Rhine Valley in Germany, sponsor Web sites. These may point you to organizations or information that don't show up in other searches. Remember, Web search engines are fallible; they don't find every site you need.

- **Why** is the information you're searching for important? The answer to this question can lead you to related fields. New drugs, for example, are important not only to victims of diseases but to drug companies and the FDA as well.

Approach assertions you read from a skeptic's point of view. See if they stand up to critical evaluation or if you're merely emotionally attached to them. Imagine "What if . . . ?" or "What about . . . ?" scenarios that may disprove or at least call into question what you're reading. Try following each assertion you pull from the Internet with the phrase, "On the other hand. . . ." Because you can't leave the sentence hanging, you'll be forced to finish it, and this will help get you into the habit of critically examining information.

These are, of course, the same techniques critical thinkers have employed for centuries, only now you are equipped with more powerful search tools than past researchers may have ever imagined. In the time it took your antecedents to formulate their questions, you can search dozens of potential information sources. You belong to the first generation of college students to enjoy both quantity and quality in its research, along with a wider perspective on issues and the ability to form personal opinions after reasoning from a much wider knowledge base. Certainly, the potential exists for the Internet to grind out a generation of intellectual robots, "thinkers" who don't think but who regurgitate information from many sources. Technology always has its good and bad aspects. However, we also have the potential to become some of the most well-informed thinkers in the history of the world, thinkers who are not only articulate but confident that their opinions have been distilled from a range of views, processed by their own personalities, beliefs, and biases. This is one of the aspects of the Internet that makes this era such an exciting combination of humanism and technology.

part

1

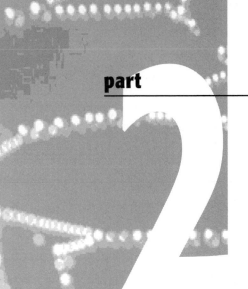

Activities and Special Education Resources on the Internet

Most of the following Web sites have been adapted for text-only use, to assist users who may be using screen readers. The sites have been organized into categories, to make it easier to find what you need.

Transition

Activity 1

Visit the School to Work Interagency Transition Partnership site.

What is the stated purpose of the site?

_____

_____

_____

What are the benefits for teachers, counselors, other school personnel or parents of the site?

_____

_____

_____

What are three ideas you have for using this site?

_____

_____

_____

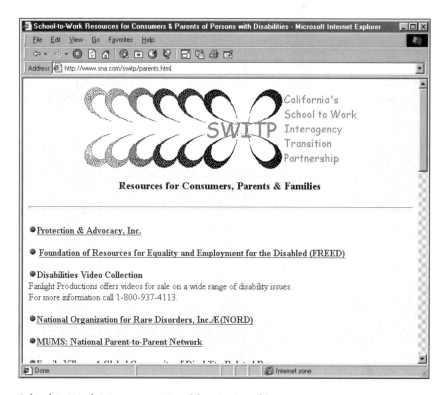

School to Work Interagency Transition Partnership

`http://www.sna.com/switp/parents.html`

Resources for consumers, parents, and families

Activity 2

Select one of your students or create a fictional case study student whose family has requested assistance with planning his or her transition from high school to the next phase of his/her life. Use the Web sites below to provide the student and the family with considerations and resources which will be helpful.

Student's Name _____

Age _____

Educational Goals following high school: _____

_____

Useful URLs: _____

Employment Goals: _____

_____

Useful URLs: _____

Independent Living Goals: _____

_____

Useful URLs: _____

Social/Recreational Goals: _____

_____

Useful URLs: _____

_____

part

2

Related Web Sites

Courage Center

http://freenet.msp.mn.us/ip/health/courage_center/
top.html

Courage Center is a nonprofit organization providing rehabilitation, enrichment, and other services for people with special needs in an effort to help them reach for their full potential in every aspect of life.

Alternative Work Concepts

http://www.teleport.com/~awc/

Alternative Work Concepts is a nonprofit employment agency for people with physical and multiple disabilities. AWC assists these people in finding jobs in their community.

National Transition Assistance for Youth with Disabilities

http://www.sna.com/swimp/parents.html

Publications, resources, searchable databases, model programs

The School-to-Work Outreach Project (STWOP)

http://www.ici.coled.umn.edu/schooltowork/

STWOP, funded by the U.S. Department of Education, tries to improve school-to-work activities including students with disabilities by sharing school-to-work models and strategies.

Pursuit

http://pursuit.rehab.uiuc.edu/pursuit/homepage.html

Pursuit encourages disabled students to pursue their academic and professional aspirations in careers in the fields of math, engineering, computers, and science.

part

2

School-to-Work National Office

http://www.stw.ed.gov/

Information on national priorities, funding, programs

National Institute on Life Planning for Persons with Disabilities

http://www.sonic.net/nilp/

Helps families with information on transition, life and person centered planning, government benefits, advocacy, guardianship, housing, supported employment

Job Accommodation Network

http://www.jan.wvu.edu/

Service of the President's Committee on Employment of People with Disabilities; publications, facts about job accommodations

Parents
Activity 1

Visit the Parents and Educators Resource Center site. If you were the parent of a middle school-age child with learning disabilities, list three resources that would be of interest to you at this site. Try out five of the links and describe each one.

Resources: _____

_____

_____

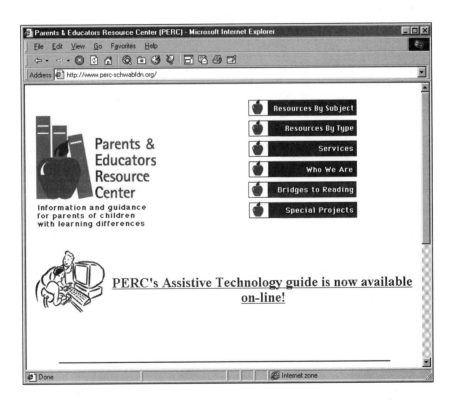

part

2

Parents and Educators Resource Center

`http://www.perc-schwabfdn.org/`

Resources by type, subject, links to other sites, publications focused primarily on learning disabilities/differences

URL: _____

Description: _____

_____

URL: _____

Description: _____

_____

URL: _____

Description: _____

_____

URL: _____

Description: _____

_____

URL: _____

Description: _____

_____

If you were a teacher of students with learning disabilities, how might this site be used to acquaint your students with the meaning of "learning disabilities"?

_____

_____

_____

_____

Activity 2

Visit the Parents Helping Parents site. What resources from this national center are available to help you as an educator? For the geographic area in which you live, to what parent resources does this site refer you?

URL: _____

Description of resources:_____

_____

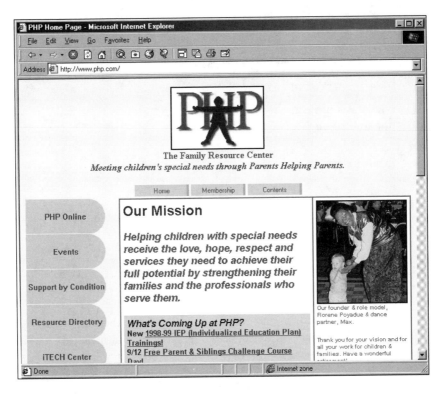

part
2

Parents Helping Parents

http://www.php.com

National parent resource center, programs, events, links

URL: _____

Description of resources:_____

_____

URL: _____

Description of resources:_____

_____

URL: _____

Description of resources:_____

_____

Related Web Sites

Child and Family Studies Program at Allegheny University

http://www.asri.edu/cfsp

Numerous projects to support families and professionals with information and resources

Family Village

http://www.familyvillage.wisc.edu

Information, resources, and communication opportunities for persons with mental retardation and other disabilities

Family & Advocates Partnership for Education (FAPE)

http://www.fape.org/

FAPE aims to inform and educate families about the Individuals with Disabilities Education Act of 1997. This site has information on FAPE's goals, a calendar, laws and regulations, associated links, and more.

Federation for Children with Special Needs

http://www.fcsn.org/home.htm

Massachusetts-based resource center for parents, projects, updates

Through the Looking Glass

http://www.lookingglass.org/

Independent living movement news, resources, conferences, links

Technical Assistance Alliance for Parent Centers

http://www.taalliance.org/

This innovative project serves families with disabled children by providing technical assistance for establishing, developing, and coordinating Parent Training and Information Projects under the Individuals with Disabilities Education Act.

part
2

Activity 3

Begin a resource file for parents who have a child with a particular disability, such as attention deficit disorder or learning disabilities. Visit the Web sites in the parent section below and list the resources available from the site.

Disability area: _____

Age of child: _____

URL: _____

Description of resources: _____

_____

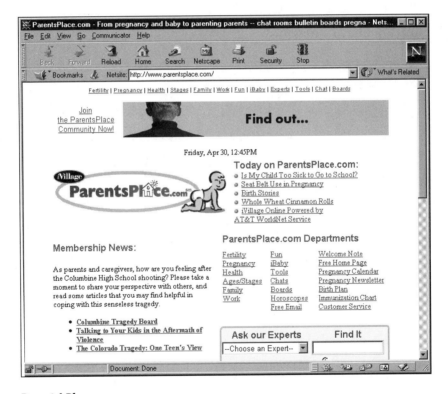

Parents' Place

```
http://www.parentsplace.com
```

News magazine of topics of interest to parents, online chat with pediatrician, bulletin boards

URL: _____

Description of resources: _____

_____

URL: _____

Description of resources: _____

_____

URL: _____

Description of resources: _____

_____

URL: _____

Description of resources: _____

_____

part 2

URL: _____

Description of resources: _____

_____

URL: _____

Description of resources: _____

_____

URL: _____

Description of resources: _____

_____

Related Web Sites

Family Education Network

http://familyeducation.com/index.asp

Special needs channel, newsgroup, topical stories, searchable index, links

Special Kidz Resource Network

http://www.specialkids.org/

The SpecialKidz Resource Network brings information and assistance to children with special needs. This searchable site provides news and advice for parents and teachers of special needs children.

National Parent Information Network

http://www.npin.org/

Sponsored by ERIC; parent news, searchable database

Inclusion

Activity 1

Visit the Consortium on Inclusive Schooling Practices. Select an issue related to inclusion (e.g., What kinds of curriculum and instructional strategies work best for students who are included in general education classrooms?).

Summarize the three key points of the policy paper.

_____

_____

_____

What are three ways you might use such a policy paper?

_____

_____

_____

part

2

Related Web Sites

Institute on Community Integration

http://www.ici.coled.umn.edu/ici/

Research, training, publications, resources

The New York Institute for Special Education (NYISE)

http://www.nyise.org/college.htm

NYISE has collected links to many universities that offer programs for the disabled.

LD Online

http://www.ldonline.org/

This interactive guide to learning disabilities for parents, students and teachers offers newsletters, teaching tips, and more.

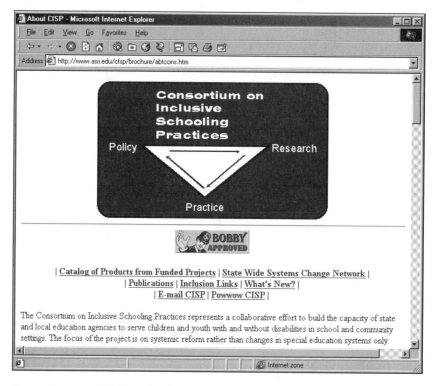

Consortium on Inclusive Schooling Practices

http://www.asri.edu/cfsp/brochure/abtcons.htm

Issue briefs, policy papers, information on policy reform, capacity building, and knowledge dissemination

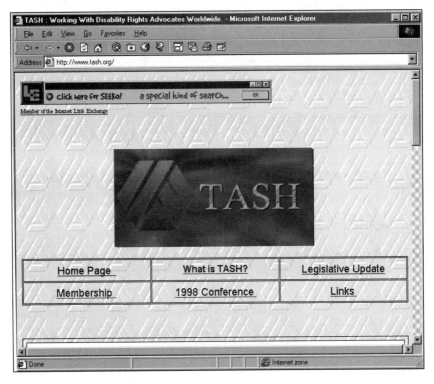

The Association for Persons with Severe Disabilities

http://www.tash.org

Conference, newsletter, discussion groups

Activity 2

Imagine that you are trying to help parents evaluate the benefits of an inclusive setting for their child. Your school administration is also unclear as to the capabilities of your school site to offer such a placement.

Brief description of child and learning needs and strengths: _____

_____

_____

_____

Site that offers suggestions for families in deciding on placement options for their child:

_____

Site that offers suggestions and resources for schools/teachers who are considering inclusion:

_____

Site that offers research on outcomes of inclusive settings:

_____

Related Web Sites

Interwork Institute

http://interwork.sdsu.edu/

The home page of the Interwork Institute, an organization working to enable communities to support members with disabilities, includes information about group projects and resources.

Disability Resources

Activity 1

Visit the SERI site. Imagine that you are a special education teacher who is trying to help a general education include a student with Asperger's Syndrome. List the links that will help this teacher and start a resource file for yourself for the future with information related to Asperger's.

URL: _____

Description:_____

_____

URL: _____

Description:_____

_____

part

2

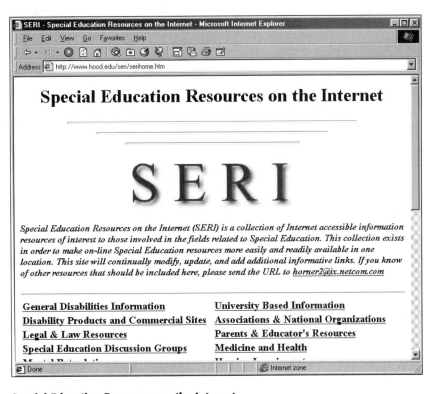

Special Education Resources on the Internet

http://www.hood.edu/seri/serihome.htm

Comprehensive disability-specific, topical, lists and links

URL: _____

Description:_____

_____

URL: _____

_____

Description:_____

_____

URL: _____

Description:_____

_____

Related Web Sites

American Council of the Blind (ACB)

http://www.acb.org/

ACB strives to improve the well-being of all blind and visually impaired people. This site offers *The Braille Forum* (a free monthly magazine), forums, helpful resources, radio, programs and more.

Internet Special Education Resources

http://www.iser.com

Nationwide directory of professionals who serve learning disabilities and special education communities in assessment, placements, therapy, advocacy

Office of Special Education Programs (U.S. Department of Education)

part

2

http://www.ed.gov/offices/OSERS/OSEP/index.html

OSEP provides leadership and fiscal resources to assist state and local efforts to educate children with disabilities. This site provides information about the agency, its programs and publications, and links to related sites.

The Schwab Foundation for Learning

http://www.schwablearning.org/

This foundation offers a wide range of services and information to support and promote the lives of children with learning differences.

The National Information Center for Children and Youth with Disabilities (NICHCY)

http://www.nichcy.org/

NICHCY is the national information and referral center that provides information on disabilities and disability-related issues for families, educators, and other professionals.

Net Connections for Communication Disorders and Sciences

http://www.mankato.msus.edu/dept/comdis/kuster2/
welcome.html

The National Clearinghouse for Professions in Special Education (NCPSE)

http://www.specialedcareers.org/

NCPSE, an information resource for professionals and potential students in the fields of special education and related professions, gathers and disseminates information on recruitment, pre-service preparation, employment opportunities, and more.

Learning Disabilities On-Line

http://www.ldonline.org

Resources, essays, audio clips from experts, online newsletter

Lupus Foundation of America (LFA)

http://www.lupus.org/lupus/index.html

LFA is dedicated to improving detection methods for lupus. This is done through increased awareness, alleviation of suffering through service and support, and the eradication of lupus through research.

Down Syndrome WWW Page

http://www.downsyndrome.com

Organizations, support groups, inclusion and education resources, family essays, events, and conferences

Illinois Assistive Technology Project

http://www.iltech.org/

IATP is a federally mandated program that provides information and services related to assistive technology for disabled individuals.

Librarian's Guide to the Best Information on the Net

http://www.sau.edu/cwis/internet/wild/disabled/
disindex.htm

Categories of resources, links

Hearing, Speech, and Deafness Center

http://www.hsdc.org/

HSDC is a fully accredited independent agency that offers services to

part

2

help people with communication problems related to hearing loss and/or speech and language impairments. This site contains information on services, programs, and a store.

National Center for Learning Disabilities, Inc.

http://www.ncld.org/

News, links, resources for families and professionals

Allyn & Bacon

http://www.abacon.com/education/specialed/spedhome.html

Textbooks, instructional resources

Disability Net

http://www.disabilitynet.co.uk

News items, advertising, services, discussion groups

Council on Education of the Deaf

http://www.educ.kent.edu/deafed/

Curriculum materials, instructional strategies, job board, teacher preparation programs

Internet Resources for Special Children

http://www.irsc.org/

National Fathers Network (NFN)

http://www.fathersnetwork.org/mn/index1.html

NFN, a nonprofit organization providing support and resources to fathers and families with special needs children, provides articles, resources, links, and a photo album at their site.

Avenues to Independence

http://www.avenuestoindependence.org/

This nonprofit, charitable organization provides programs and assistance to help developmentally disabled individuals increase independence.

Dreamms for Kids

http://www.dreamms.org/

This assistive technology information clearinghouse is committed to increasing the use of computers and assistive technologies for students with special needs. This site has articles and products for special needs.

Learning Disabilities Association of California

http://www.ldaca.org/

The group works to advance understanding of the education of children with learning disabilities and to increase community awareness and acceptance of persons with learning disabilities and their families.

Special Needs Network

http://www.schoolnet.ca/sne/

Canada's Special Needs Education project, links, discussion groups

Closing the Gap

http://www.closingthegap.com/

Resource Guide, newspaper, articles, conferences

part

2

Activity 2

Imagine that you are a teacher of preschool students with physical disabilities. Parents of your students are planning for the holidays and request your help locating appropriate toys. Use the Toy Catalog site to help find five toy producers whose catalogs you would want to review.

URL: _____

Description:_____

_____

URL: _____

Description:_____

_____

URL: _____

Description: _____

_____

URL: _____

Description: _____

_____

URL: _____

Description: _____

_____

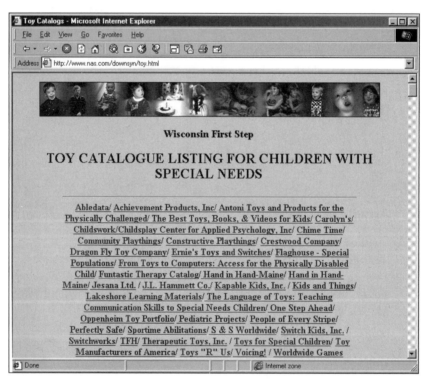

Toy Catalog Listing for Children with Special Needs

```
http://www.nas.com/downsyn/toy.html
```

Toys listed by title, links to producers; mailing list

Related Web Sites

Special Olympics International

http://www.specialolympics.org

Programs, magazine

National Association for the Mentally Ill

http://www.nami.org/medical.htm

News, research, resources, helpline, books, topical information

Activity 3

Visit the CEC site. Find out what training resources are available on the new IDEA legislation.

_____

_____

_____

part

2

Imagine that you are a special educator interested in moving to a new state. What employment opportunities are available there?

State to which you want to move:

_____

Jobs available there:

_____

_____

_____

Related Web Sites

Center for the Study of Autism

http://www.autism.org

Subgroups, issues, interventions, overview in different languages

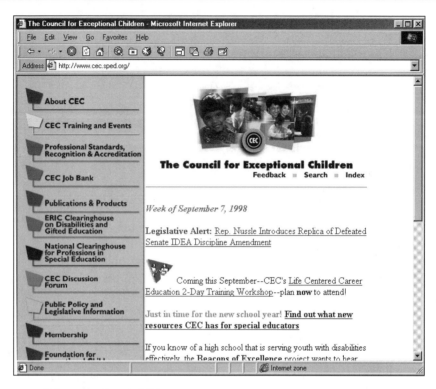

Council for Exceptional Children

http://www.cec.sped.org

Discussion forum, job bank, public policy/legislative information, variety of disabilities/issues

National Federation for the Blind

http://www.nfb.org

Links to news, events, research, jobline, resources

part

2

Technology

Activity 1

Visit the ATA site. Find the resource center nearest you and determine what services they could provide which would enhance your program.

_____

_____

_____

_____

part

2

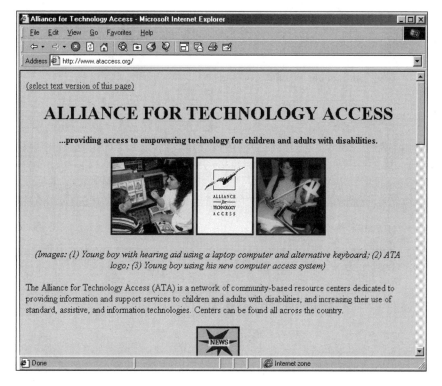

Alliance for Technology Access

`http://www.ataccess.org`

Grassroots national organization to provide information/resources to parents and professionals on disabilities and technology

Related Web Sites

CHADD

`http://www.chadd.org`

Children and Adults with Attention Deficit Disorder support group and information/resources

Down Syndrome Support Group and Information/Resources Network

`http://www.nas.com/downsyn`

The Center for Information Technology Accommodation (CITA)

`http://www.itpolicy.gsa.gov/cita/nii.htm`

CITA and the National Information Infrastructure (NII) Task Force participate in initiatives to ensure that the NII will be accessible to users with disabilities.

part

2

The Training and Technical Assistance Center (T-TAC)

`http://tac.elps.vt.edu/`

T-TAC strives to improve educational opportunities and contribute to the success of children and youth with disabilities by providing training and technical assistance.

The Association for Retarded Citizens

`http://www.thearc.org`

Support group and information/resources network for families and professionals working in the field of mental retardation.

Developmental Disabilities Resource Center

`http://www.ddrcco.com`

Activity 2

Imagine that you are trying to increase the access for your students to technology in the classroom. Searching the Web sites listed below, find out which sites provide you with strategies, information on benefits and outcomes, funding sources, and technical assistance.

Name and URL of site: _____

Type of information: _____

_____

Name and URL of site: _____

Type of information: _____

_____

Name and URL of site: _____

Type of information: _____

_____

Name and URL of site: _____

Type of information: _____

_____

Name and URL of site: _____

Type of information: _____

_____

part

2

Related Web Sites

Technology and Media Division of the Council for Exceptional Children

`http://www.ucc.uconn.edu/~tam`

Publications, links, conferences

Government

Activity 1

You want to do some research in your classroom about the effectiveness of a particular strategy on learning outcomes. Visit the government sites listed below and find some sites that will help you select a specific grant to apply for.

Focus of research project: _____

_____

Site with grant information appropriate for my project:

_____

Site with grant information appropriate for my project:

_____

Site with grant information appropriate for my project:

_____

Site with grant information appropriate for my project:

_____

part

2

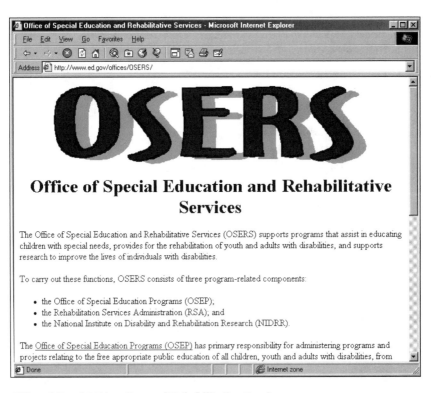

Office of Special Education and Rehabilitative Services

http://www.ed.gov/offices/OSERS/

Information on programs and services

Related Web Sites

U.S. Government Printing Office (Federal Register, public laws, etc.)

http://www.access.gpo.gov/su_docs/

Federal Resource Center for Special Education

http://www.dssc.org/frc/

Technical assistance project, publications, conferences

The Office of Special Education Programs (OSEP)

http://www.ed.gov/offices/OSERS/OSEP/osep.html

OSEP is a component of the Office of Special Education and Rehabilitative Services (OSERS). This site offers information on special education projects and funding.

The National Center to Improve Practice (NCIP)

http://www.edc.org/FSC/NCIP/

NCIP promotes the use of technology to enhance the education of students with disabilities. Review the organization's library, watch video profiles, and go on a tour of two exemplary early childhood classrooms.

Americans with Disabilities Act Document Center

http://janweb.icdi.wvu.edu/kinder/

This site contains copies of the Americans with Disabilities Act of 1990, ADA regulations, technical assistance manuals prepared by the U.S. Equal Employment Opportunity Commission (EEOC) and other disability-related documents from the US government.

The National Institute on Disability and Rehabilitation Research (NIDRR)

http://www.ed.gov/offices/OSERS/NIDRR/index.html

This site offers information programs at NIDRR, a calendar of events, and an organization chart.

National Information Center for Children and Youth with Disabilities

http://www.nichcy.org

Publications in English and Spanish, news, posters, search for organizations

part

2

Curriculum/Strategies/Interventions

Activity 1

Have your students visit the Blue Mountain Arts Web site and send a greeting card to a friend or family member.

Describe the card.

_____

_____

_____

How could you use this site with students? Describe three activities related to language arts/reading, mathematics, and science that would be appropriate for the grade level, age, and disabilities of the students with whom you work.

_____

_____

_____

_____

Related Web Sites

Dyslexia: The Gift

http://www.dyslexia.com/

This searchable site with information about dyslexia includes curriculum aids for teachers with dyslexic students, a bookstore, a discussion board, and links.

Blue Web'n Learning Applications

http://www.kn.pacbell.com/wired/bluewebn

Sponsored by PacBell; lesson plans and teaching resources

Blue Mountain Arts

`http://www.bluemountain.com`

Send personalized greeting cards free to friends and relatives

Education World

`http://www.education-world.com`

Searchable database of more than 50,000 sites related to curriculum ideas and hot picks of the week

The Special Needs Education (SNE) project

`http://www.schoolnet.ca/sne/`

The SNE project is an Internet-based service that provides resources in educating students with special needs to parents, teachers, schools, and others.

The Association for Supervision and Curriculum Development (ASCD)

http://www.ascd.org/

ASCD, a non-profit international education association, is committed offering guidelines in teaching and learning for the success of all students. This site offers information on membership, forums, educational issues, and more.

Kathy Schrock's Guide for Educators

http://www.capecod.net/schrockguide

Classified list of sites useful for enhancing curriculum and professional growth, updated daily

National Geographic

http://www.nationalgeographic.com

Constantly changing sites, projects, and information

Yahooligans

http://www.yahooligans.com

Child-safe search engine, links, discussion groups

part
2

Activity 2

Visit the Regional Technology Education Consortium page at **http://rtec.org** and find a software review for a piece of software that would be appropriate for one of the students with whom you work.

Software Title and Publisher: _____

_____

Description:_____

_____

_____

_____

_____

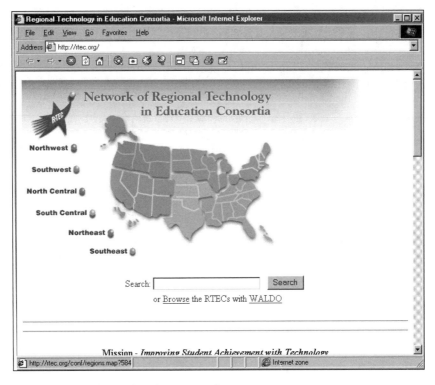

Regional Technology Education Consortium

http://rtec.org

Links to the six regional technology consortia established to help states, districts, and schools use technology to support improved teaching and student achievement

Related Web Sites

Developing Educational Standards

http://www.putwest.boces.org/standards.html

This page acts as a repository for as much information about educational standards and curriculum frameworks from all sources (national, state, local, and other) as can be found on the Internet.

Mid-Continent Regional Educational Library (McREL)

http://www.mcrel.org/

McREL's goal is to make a difference in the quality of education and learning through applied research, product development, and service. This site provides resources and lesson plans for educators as well as information on educational standards.

Activity 3

Visit the Math Forum site and select a lesson plan that would be appropriate for your students.

Title of Lesson: _____

Objectives:

_____

_____

Grade Level: _____

Brief Description:

_____

_____

_____

_____

Related Web Sites

PlaneMath

http://www.planemath.com/

InfoUse with NASA provides student activities in math and aeronautics.

Science Teachers Enhancement Model (STEM)

http://www.nyu.edu/projects/mstep/menu.html

STEM's goal is to increase the performance and skills of K–12 students in the areas of science and math. This site provides lesson plans, activities, and information for math and science teachers.

American Mathematical Society (AMS)

http://e-math.ams.org/

The AMS works to further mathematical research and scholarship by in-

The Math Forum

`http://forum.swarthmore.edu/index.js.html`

Searchable database of math lesson plans by topic and grade level, issues, resources

creasing the awareness of the value of math to society and fostering high standards in math education. This site offers educational math-related information and products.

Eisenhower National Clearinghouse

`http://www.enc.org`

Variety of math and science lessons for grades 4–12; publications, services

Family Math Home Page

`http://theory.lcs.mit.edu:80/~emjordan/famMath.html`

K–6 math program; activities

Activity 4

Visit Carol Hurst's Web site and select a book title and activity that will be appropriate in your classroom or program. Describe it below.

Curriculum Theme: _____

Title and Author of Book: _____

_____

Lesson Ideas:

_____

_____

_____

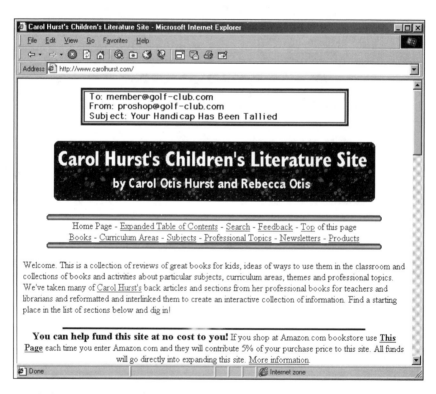

Carol Hurst's Children's Literature

http://www.carolhurst.com

Reviews of great books for students, ideas of ways to use them in the classroom, collections of books on themes, subjects, and topics

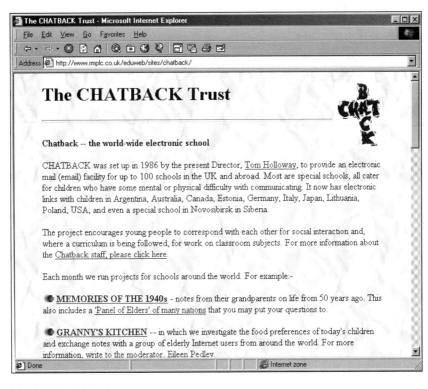

part
2

The Chatback Trust

`http://visitweb.com/chatback`

A topical Web site where students can interact with characters from history or chat with people who have connections to important historical events

Related Web Sites

Recording for the Blind and Dyslexic

`http://www.rfbd.org/`

National lending library of books on tape

Library of Congress National Library Service for the Blind and Physically Handicapped

`http://lcweb.loc.gov/nls/`

Services and programs

Language Arts Resources for Teachers

http://www.csun.edu/~vceed009/languagearts.html

The California State University at Northridge has created this collection of literature and language arts resources and lesson plans.

Activity 5

Visit the Chatback Trust and try out this site by communicating with an historical figure. Select a figure who would be appropriate to help your students learn about a significant period in history for them.

Historical figure you chose:

_____

Describe your interaction:

_____

_____

_____

part

2

Historical figure appropriate for your students:

_____

Lesson description:

_____

_____

_____

_____

_____

_____

Related Web Sites

EPA Curriculum, Resources, and Activities

http://www.epa.gov/teachers/curriculum_resources.htm

The Environmental Protection Agency offers a collection of natural science curriculum, activity information, and links to additional sites.

Cable Network Support for Teachers

Activity 1

Visit the PBS site and select an upcoming educational special that would be appropriate for your curriculum/students. What support resources are available for teachers?

Curriculum area:

_____

Title of Program:

_____

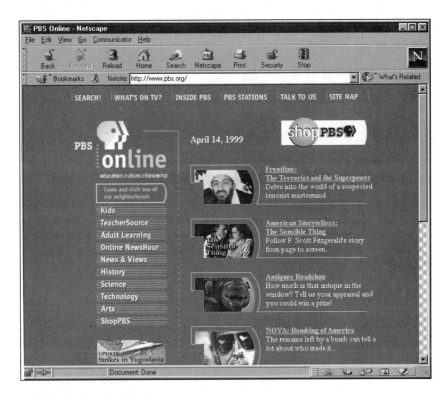

part

2

Public Broadcasting Service

http://www.pbs.org

Frequently updated, varied topics

Support materials available:

_____

_____

_____

_____

_____

_____

_____

Related Web Sites

The listings below are for cable channels that offer support materials, lesson plans, and activities found nowhere else to support teachers. The content changes frequently and new features are added all the time.

CNN Interactive

`http://www.cnn.com`

Up-to-the-minute news reports with subjects classified for search

Discovery Channel On-Line

`http://www.discovery.com`

Feature stories, expeditions, games, frequently updated

Activity 2

Visit the Jason Project site. What are the two novels for this year's project? How might you use these novels with students who have learning disabilities in an upper grade classroom studying the rain forest?

How might your students participate in the project?

_____

Names of Novels/Authors:

_____

_____

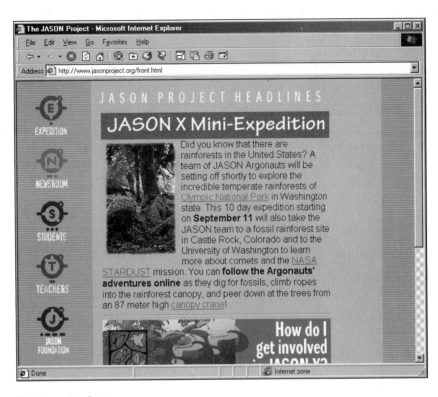

part

2

The Jason Project

`http://www.jasonproject.org/front.html`

Each year a different destination is chosen for students to interact with and learn about. This year's project is the Amazon rain forest.

Lesson Ideas:

_____

_____

_____

_____

_____

_____

_____

Related Web Sites

A&E

`http://www.aetv.com`

Lesson plans and resources

Animal Planet

`http://animal.discovery.com/animal.html`

This site provides information on the television network Animal Planet, and offers a TV schedule, information on programming, and related links.

Black Entertainment Network

`http://www.betnetworks.com`

Bravo

`http://www.bravotv.com`

Cartoon Network

`http://www.filmzone.com/SpaceGhost/cartoonnet.html`

C-SPAN

`http://www.c-span.org`

The Family Channel

`http://www.famfun.com`

Fox News

`http://www.foxnews.com`

The History Channel

`http://www.historychannel.com`

The Learning Channel

`http://www.discovery.com/educ`

Lifetime

http://www.lifetimetv.com

Showtime

http://www.showtimeonline.com

Turner Network Television

http://www.tnt-tv.com/

Travel Channel

http://www.travelchannel.com/travelhome.html

Offers information on the television network Travel Channel. Users will find a TV schedule, info on programming, and details on different travel areas in the world.

USA

http://www.usanetwork.com

The Weather Channel

http://www.weather.com/weather

part
2

Student Collaborative Projects

Classroom Connect

http://www.classroom.com

Mayaquest 98 and Africa Quest 98, along with other experiential adventures; teacher resources and lesson ideas

Virtual Field Trips

Activity 1

Visit the White House site. What are the advantages of a virtual field trip to the White House over a real-life visit? What are the disadvantages?

Advantages:

_____

_____

_____

_____

part

2

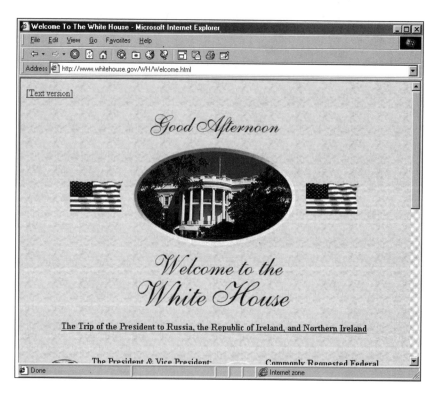

The White House

http://www.whitehouse.gov

Tour of the White House, email Washington, D.C.

Disadvantages:

_____

_____

_____

_____

_____

What are some lesson ideas to go along with your virtual field trip?

_____

_____

_____

_____

part
2

Related Web Sites

Global Schoolhouse

`http://www.gsn.org`

Activity 2

Visit the Exploratorium site. List five ideas for your classroom virtual field trip.

_____

_____

_____

_____

Related Web Sites

Big Bend National Park Virtual Field Trip

`http://www.maroon.com/bigbend/intro/index.html`

Exploratorium

http://www.exploratorium.edu

Science resources for students, parents, teachers

Take a virtual field trip of Big Bend National Park in West Texas at this site. It provides a virtual hike, images of the park, information on geological structures, and related links.

NASA's Quest Project

http://www.quest.arc.nasa.gov/

Online interactive projects

Global On-Line Adventure Learning Site

http://www.goals.com

Follow real-life adventurers as they post daily reports on their travels

Virtual Field Trips

http://www.field-guides.com/

Online field trips take the visitor to all sorts of places. Teachers' resources and guides, as well as complimentary Web sites, assist in learning about the subject area covered.

 ## Research

Activity 1

Visit the CAST site. What is universal design? Why is it so important for students with disabilities?

Universal design is . . .

_____

_____

It is important because . . .

_____

_____

part

2

Related Web Sites

John F. Kennedy Center for Research on Human Development

http://www.vanderbilt.edu/kennedy/

Research topics, training, and information dissemination on behavioral, intellectual, and brain development

Eunice Kennedy Shriver Center

http://www.shriver.org/

This site provides research, education, and services information about mental retardation.

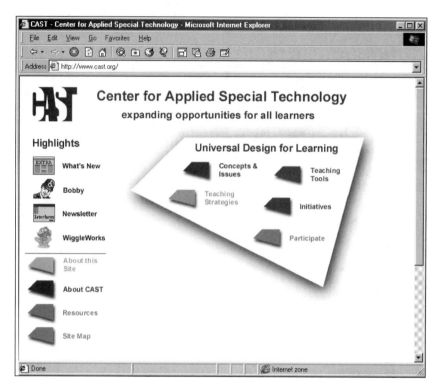

Center for Applied Special Technology

http://www.cast.org

Resources, links, information on universal design research

The Instant Access Treasure Chest

http://www.fln.vcu.edu/ld/ld.html

This site has collected links to disability-related sites, articles, and resources. This is a great place to start any research on disabilities.

National Center to Improve Practice

http://www.edc.org/FSC/NCIP

Resources, links, online conferencing on issues in special education and technology

Activity 2

Visit the ERIC site. Find a lesson plan that would be appropriate for your students. List its site.

Select a topic related to a specific disability or issue in special education for a library search. How many articles did you find?

How does the ERIC search help you with your work as a teacher?

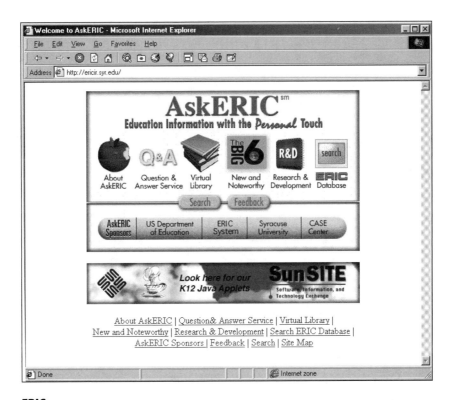

ERIC

`http://ericir.syr.edu`

Literature searches, lesson plans, links to numerous useful sites

Related Web Sites

Trace Center

http://www.trace.wisc.edu

Information and links on assistive technology devices and software

 ## Assistive Techology Hardware and Software

Activity 1

Visit the IntelliTools site. What is an overlay?

_____

_____

part
2

Print out an overlay and a lesson and describe how you might use them with your students.

_____

_____

_____

_____

_____

_____

_____

Related Web Sites

Virtual Assistive Technology Center (VATC)

http://www.at-center.com/

VATC offers free assistive technology software in an effort to put computers within reach of people with disabilities.

Tools for Life Assistive Technology

http://www2.gasou.edu/tools/tools.htm

ABLEDATA

http://www.abledata.com

Sponsored by the National Institute on Disability and Rehabilitation Research; searchable database on adaptive devices, news, links

This site from Georgia Southern University offers information on adaptive toys, aids for daily living, and other assistive technologies.

Apple Computer Disability Home Page

http://www2.apple.com/disability/default.html

Lots of useful links, resources

WebABLE!

http://www.webable.com/

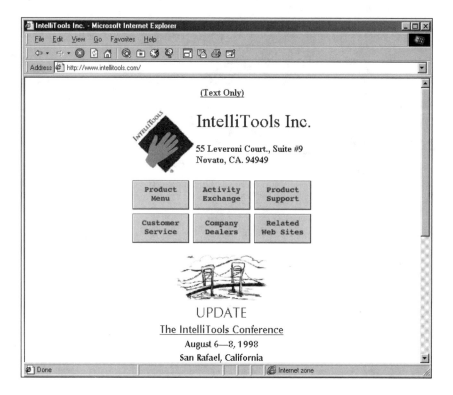

IntelliTools

`http://www.intellitools.com`

Producers of assistive devices and software; overlay activity exchange; useful links

WebABLE! is dedicated to stimulating education, and research and development of technologies that will assist disabled people in accessing information systems and emerging technologies. Search the database to find links to many related sites.

Activity 2

Parents of a student who has severe difficulties with keyboarding and spelling want to investigate speech input as an alternative for his writing assignments. What options for speech input word processing are listed in the ABLEDATA database?

_____

_____

_____

_____

What resources does the Center for Accessible Technology provide for evaluating the advantages and disadvantages for the different systems? Visit their site (**http://www.wl.net/CAT/**) to find out.

_____

_____

_____

_____

_____

part

2

Related Web Sites

LAB Resources

`http://www.execpc.com/~labres/`

LAB Resources focuses on assistive technology in designing computer software and hardware especially for special needs and education.

Assistive Technology On-Line Main Menu

`http://www.asel.udel.edu/at-online/assistive.html`

Comprehensive, searchable resources in AT; funding, organizations, research, policy, glossary, devices, and services

Don Johnston Inc.

`http://www.donjohnston.com/`

Software, assistive technology devices, classroom tips, technology tips

Listing of Special Education URLs

Transition

http://www.sna.com/switp/parents.html

http://www.stw.ed.gov/

http://www.sonic.net/nilp/

http://www.jan.wvu.edu/

http://www.ici.coled.umn.edu/schooltowork/

http://www.teleport.com/~awc/

http://freenet.msp.mn.us/ip/health/courage_center/
      top.html

http://pursuit.rehab.uiuc.edu/pursuit/homepage.html

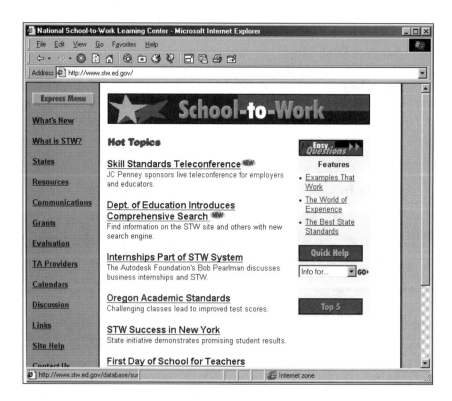

part

2

Parents

http://www.perc-schwabfdn.org/

http://www.familyvillage.wisc.edu

http://www.fcsn.org/home.htm

http://www.lookingglass.org/

http://www.php.com

http://familyeducation.com/index.asp

http://www.specialkids.org/

http://www.parentsplace.com

http://www.npin.org/

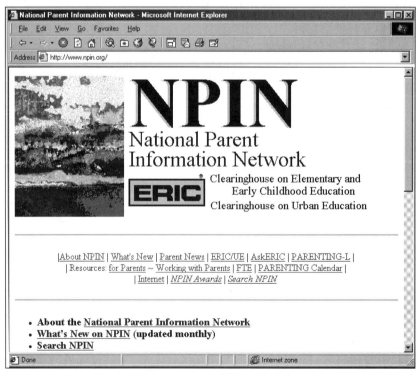

http://www.asri.edu/cfsp

http://www.fape.org/

http://www.taalliance.org/

Inclusion

http://www.ici.coled.umn.edu/ici/

http://www.asri.edu/cfsp/brochure/abtcons.htm

http://www.tash.org

http://interwork.sdsu.edu/

http://www.nyise.org/college.htm

http://www.ldonline.org/

part
2

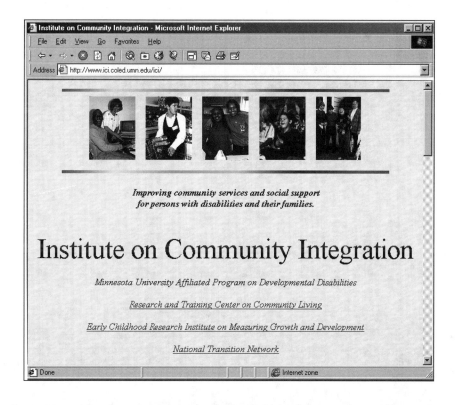

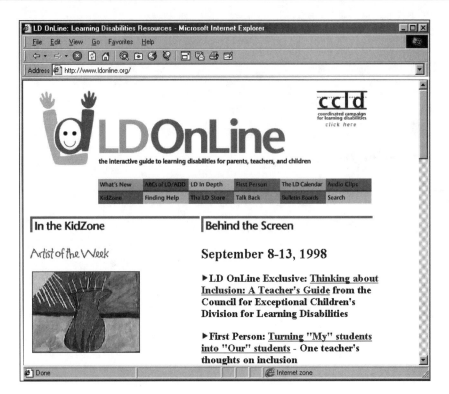

Disability Resources

http://www.iser.com

http://www.ed.gov/offices/OSERS/OSEP/index.html

http://www.schwablearning.org/

http://www.mankato.msus.edu/dept/comdis/kuster2/
    welcome.html

http://www.ldonline.org

http://www.downsyndrome.com

http://www.iltech.org/

http://www.sau.edu/cwis/internet/wild/disabled/
    disindex.htm

http://www.hsdc.org/

http://www.ncld.org/

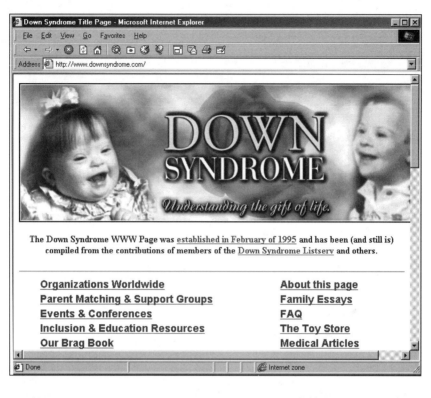

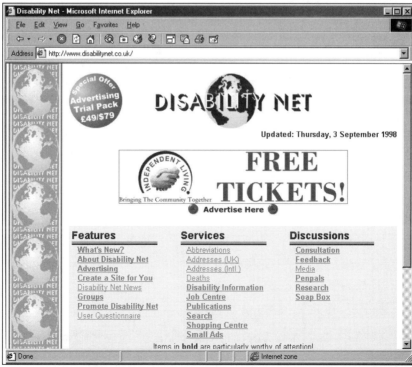

part

2

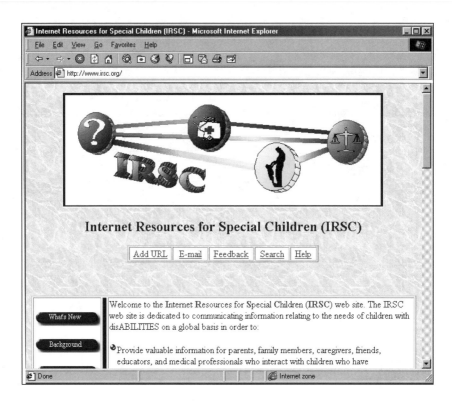

http://www.abacon.com/education/specialed/
    spedhome.html

http://www.disabilitynet.co.uk

http://www.educ.kent.edu/deafed/

http://www.irsc.org/

http://www.ucpa.org/html1/

http://www.avenuestoindependence.org/

http://www.dreamms.org/

http://www.ldaca.org/

http://www.schoolnet.ca/sne/

http://www.closingthegap.com/

http://www.hood.edu/seri/serihome.htm

http://www.specialolympics.org

http://www.nami.org/medical.htm

http://www.nas.com/downsyn//toy.html

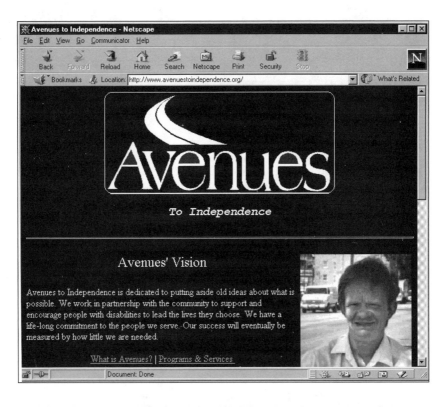

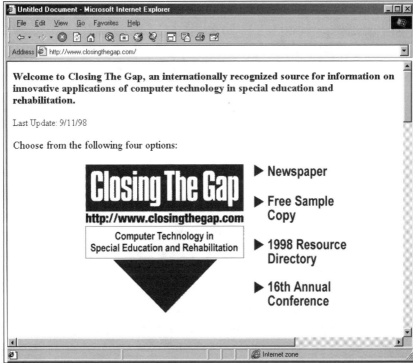

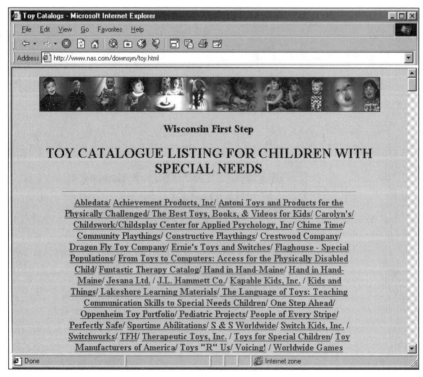

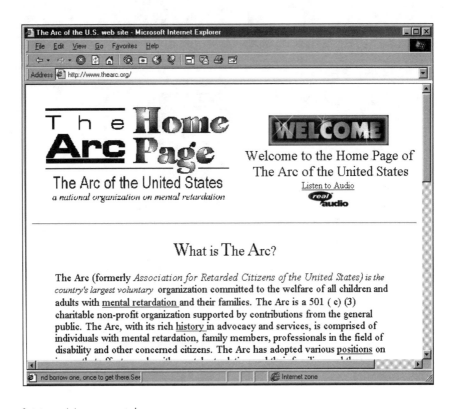

http://www.autism.org

http://www.nfb.org

http://www.cec.sped.org

http://www.chadd.org

http://www.nas.com/downsyn

http://www.thearc.org

http://www.ddrcco.com

http://www.ataccess.org

http://www.ucc.uconn.edu/~tam

http://www.acb.org/

http://www.nichcy.org/

http://www.specialedcareers.org/

http://www.lupus.org/lupus/index.html

part

2

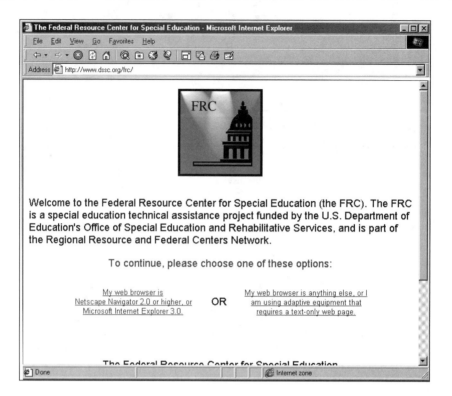

part
2

Government

http://www.access.gpo.gov/su_docs/

http://www.dssc.org/frc/

http://www.nichcy.org

http://www.ed.gov/offices/OSERS/

http://www.ed.gov/offices/OSERS/OSEP/osep.html

http://www.edc.org/FSC/NCIP/

http://janweb.icdi.wvu.edu/kinder/

http://www.ed.gov/offices/OSERS/NIDRR/index.html

Curriculum/Strategies/Interventions

http://www.dyslexia.com/

http://www.bluemountain.com

http://utopia.knoware.nl/users/gentle/

http://www.planemath.com/

http://forum.swarthmore.edu/index.js.html

http://www.rfbd.org/

http://lcweb.loc.gov/nls/

http://www.carolhurst.com

http://www.schoolnet.ca/sne/

part

2

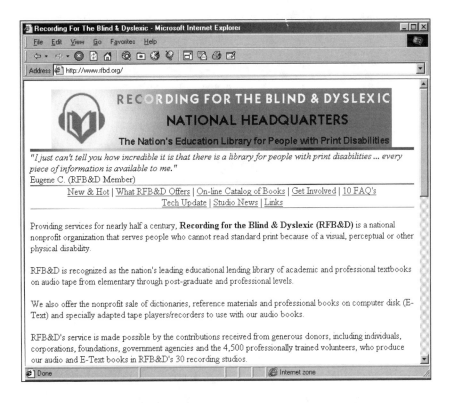

http://www.ascd.org/

http://www.eduplace.com/rdg/itl/index.html

http://visitweb.com/chatback

http://www.csun.edu/~vceed009/languagearts.html

http://www.nyu.edu/projects/mstep/menu.html

http://e-math.ams.org/

http://www.enc.org

http://theory.lcs.mit.edu:80/~emjordan/famMath.html

http://www.kn.pacbell.com/wired/bluewebn

http://www.putwest.boces.org/standards.html

http://rtec.org

http://www.education-world.com

http://www.capecod.net/schrockguide

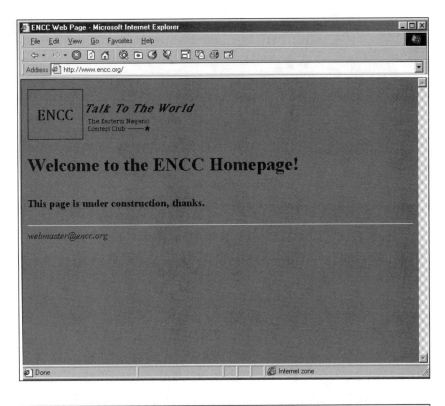

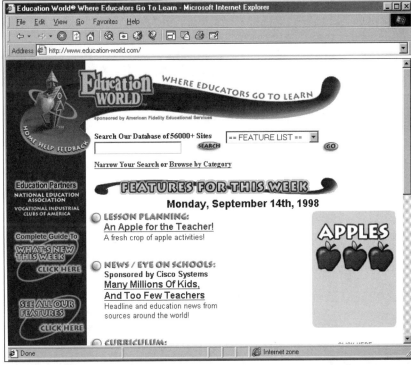

http://www.mcrel.org/

http://www.nationalgeographic.com

http://www.yahooligans.com

Cable Network Support for Teachers

http://www.cnn.com

http://www.discovery.com

http://www.pbs.org

http://www.aetv.com

http://www.betnetworks.com

http://www.bravotv.com

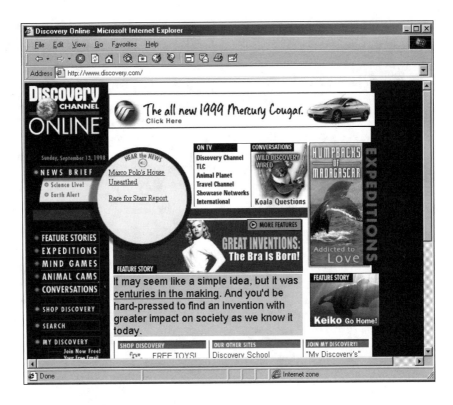

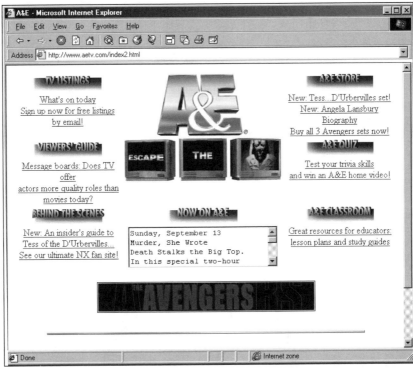

http://www.filmzone.com/SpaceGhost/cartoonnet.html

http://www.c-span.org

http://www.famfun.com

http://www.foxnews.com

http://www.historychannel.com

http://www.discovery.com/educ

http://www.lifetimetv.com

http://www.tnt-tv.com/

http://www.showtimeonline.com

http://www.usanetwork.com

http://www.weather.com/weather

http://www.travelchannel.com/travelhome.html

http://animal.discovery.com/animal.html

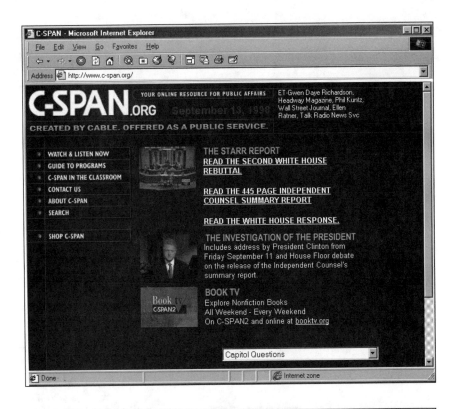

part

2

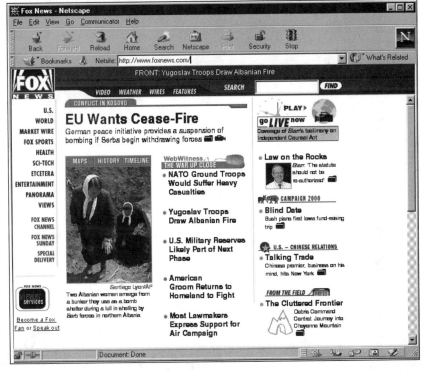

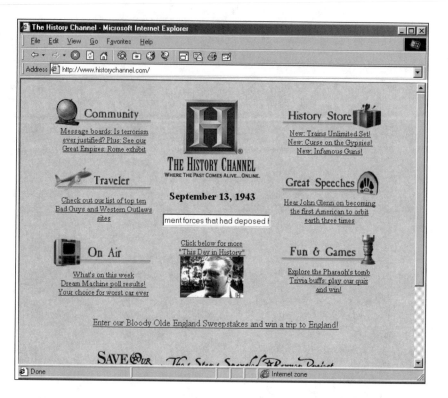

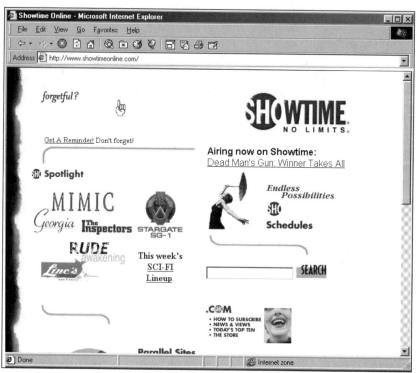

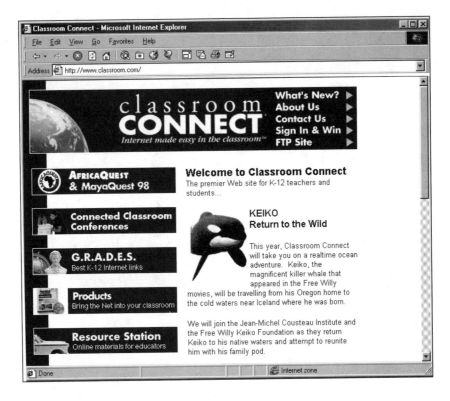

Student Collaborative Projects

http://www.classroom.com

http://www.jasonproject.org/front.html

Virtual Field Trips

http://www.gsn.org

http://www.whitehouse.gov

http://www.exploratorium.edu

http://www.quest.arc.nasa.gov/

http://www.goals.com

part

2

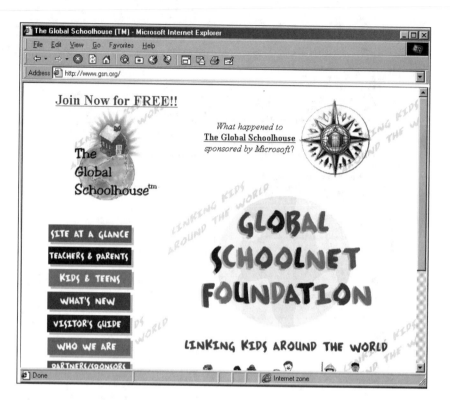

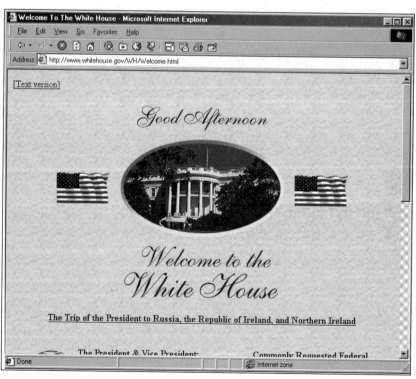

```
http://www.maroon.com/bigbend/intro/index.html
http://www.field-guides.com/
```

Research

```
http://www.vanderbilt.edu/kennedy/

http://www.shriver.org/

http://www.edc.org/FSC/NCIP

http://www.cast.org

http://www.trace.wisc.edu

http://ericir.syr.edu

http://www.asri.edu/cfsp

http://www.cast.org/

http://www.fln.vcu.edu/ld/ld.html
```

part

2

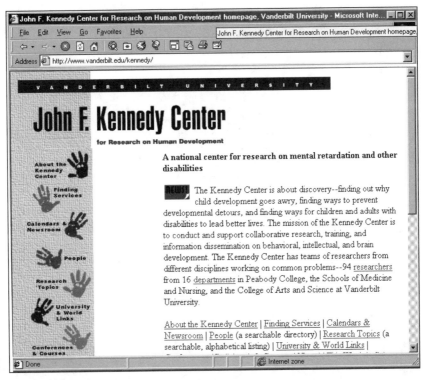

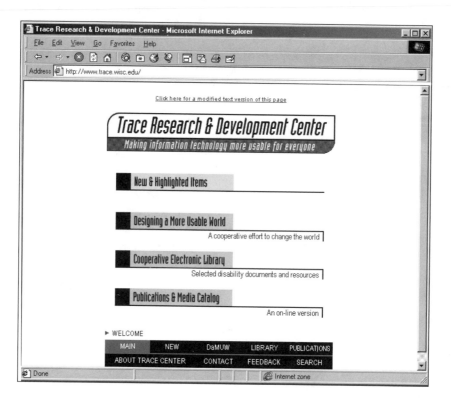

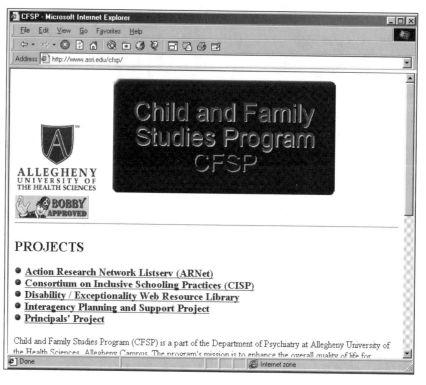

Assistive Techology Hardware and Software

http://www2.gasou.edu/tools/tools.htm

http://www2.apple.com/disability/default.html

http://www.intellitools.com

http://www.execpc.com/~labres/

http://www.asel.udel.edu/at-online/assistive.html

http://www.donjohnston.com/

http://www.abledata.com

http://www.at-center.com/

http://www.webable.com/

part
2

Documentation

Your Citation for Exemplary Research

There's another detail left for us to handle—the formal citing of electronic sources in academic papers. The very factor that makes research on the Internet exciting is the same factor that makes referencing these sources challenging: their dynamic nature. A journal article exists, either in print or on microfilm, virtually forever. A document on the Internet can come, go, and change without warning. Because the purpose of citing sources is to allow another scholar to retrace your argument, a good citation allows a reader to obtain information from your primary sources, to the extent possible. This means you need to include not only information on when a source was posted on the Internet (if available) but also when you obtained the information.

The two arbiters of form for academic and scholarly writing are the Modern Language Association (MLA) and the American Psychological Association (APA); both organizations have established styles for citing electronic publications.

MLA Style

In the second edition of the *MLA Style Manual,* the MLA recommends the following formats:

- URLs: URLs are enclosed in angle brackets (<>) and contain the access mode identifier, the formal name for such indicators as "http" or "ftp." If a URL must be split across two lines, break it only after a slash (/). Never introduce a hyphen at the end of the first line. The URL should include all the parts necessary to identify uniquely the file/document being cited.

    ```
    <http://www.csun.edu/~rtvfdept/home/index.html>
    ```

- A complete online reference contains the title of the project or database (underlined); the name of the editor of the project or database (if given); electronic publication information, including version number (if relevant and if not part of the title); date of electronic publication or latest update; name of any sponsoring institution or organization; date of access; and electronic address.

- If you cannot find some of the information, then include the information that is available.

The MLA also recommends that you print or download electronic documents, freezing them in time for future reference.

World Wide Web Site The elements of a proper citation are the name of the person creating the site (reversed), followed by a period, the title of the site (underlined), or, if there is no title, a description such as home page (such a description is neither placed in quotes nor underlined). Then specify the name of any school, organization, or other institution affiliated with the site and follow it with your date of access and the URL of the page.

```
Gotthoffer, Doug. RTVF Dept. Website. California
    State University, Northridge. 1 September 1998.
```

Some electronic references are truly unique to the online domain. These include email, newsgroup postings, MUDs (multiuser domains) or MOOs (multiuser domains, object oriented), and IRCs (Internet Relay Chats).

Email In citing email messages, begin with the writer's name (reversed) followed by a period, then the title of the message (if any) in quotations as it appears in the subject line. Next comes a description of the message, typically "Email to," and the recipient (e.g., "the author"), and finally the date of the message.

```
Davis, Jeffrey. "Web Writing Resources." Email to
     Nora Davis. 5 July 1998.

Sommers, Laurice. "Re: College Admissions Practices."
     Email to the author. 12 August 1998.
```

List Servers and Newsgroups In citing these references, begin with the author's name (reversed) followed by a period. Next include the title of the document (in quotes) from the subject line, followed by the words "Online posting" (not in quotes). Follow this with the date of posting. For list servers, include the date of access, the name of the list (if known), and the online address of the list's moderator or administrator. For newsgroups, follow "Online posting" with the date of posting, the date of access, and the name of the newsgroup, prefixed with news: and enclosed in angle brackets.

```
Applebaum, Dale. "Educational Variables." Online
     posting. 29 Jan. 1998. Higher Education
     Discussion Group. 30 January 1993
     <jlucidoj@unc.edu>.

Gostl, Jack. "Re: Mr. Levitan." Online posting.
     13 June 1997. 20 June 1997
     <news:alt.edu.bronxscience>.
```

MUDs, MOOs, and IRCs Citations for these online sources take the form of the name of the speaker(s) followed by a period. Then comes the description and date of the event, the name of the forum, the date of access, and the online address prefixed by "telnet://".

part

2

Guest. Personal interview. 13 August 1998
    <telnet//du.edu 8888>.

APA Style

The *Publication Manual of the American Psychological Association* (4th ed.) is fairly dated in its handling of online sources, having been published before the rise of the WWW and the generally recognized format for URLs. The format that follows is based on the APA manual, with modifications proposed by Russ Dewey <www.psychwww.com/resource/apacrib.htm>. It's important to remember that, unlike the MLA, the APA does not include temporary or transient sources (e.g., letters, phone calls, etc.) in its "References" page, preferring to handle them in in-text citations exclusively. This rule holds for electronic sources as well: email, MOOs/MUDs, list server postings, etc., are not included in the "References" page, merely cited in text, for example, "But Wilson has rescinded his earlier support for these policies" (Charles Wilson, personal email to the author, 20 November 1996). But also note that many list server and Usenet groups and MOOs actually archive their correspondences, so that there is a permanent site (usually a Gopher or FTP server) where those documents reside. In that case, you would want to find the archive and cite it as an unchanging source. Strictly speaking, according to the APA manual, a file from an FTP site should be referenced as follows:

Deutsch, P. (1991). "Archie-An electronic directory
    service for the Internet" [Online]. Available
    FTP: ftp.sura.net Directory: pub/archie/docs
    File: whatis.archie.

However, the increasing familiarity of Net users with the convention of a URL makes the prose description of how to find a file <"Available FTP: ftp.sura.net Directory: pub/archie/docs File: whatis.archie"> unnecessary. Simply specifying the URL should be enough.

So, with such a modification of the APA format, citations from the standard Internet sources would appear as follows.

FTP (File Transfer Protocol) Sites To cite files available for downloading via FTP, give the author's name (if known), the publication date (if available and if different from the date accessed), the full title of the paper (capitalizing only the first word and proper nouns), the address of

part

2

the FTP site along with the full path necessary to access the file, and the date of access.

```
Deutsch, P. (1991) "Archie-An electronic directory
    service for the Internet." [Online]. Available:
    ftp://ftp.sura.net/pub/archie/docs/whatis.archie.
```

WWW Sites (World Wide Web) To cite files available for viewing or downloading via the World Wide Web, give the author's name (if known), the year of publication (if known and if different from the date accessed), the full title of the article, and the title of the complete work (if applicable) in italics. Include any additional information (such as versions, editions, or revisions) in parentheses immediately following the title. Include the full URL (the http address) and the date of visit.

```
Burka, L. P. (1993). A hypertext history of multi-
    user dungeons. MUDdex. http://www.utopia.com/
    talent/lpb/muddex/essay/ (13 Jan. 1997).

Tilton, J. (1995). Composing good HTML (Vers. 2.0.6).
    http://www.cs.cmu.edu/~tilt/cgh/ (1 Dec. 1996).
```

part

2

Telnet Sites List the author's name or alias (if known), the date of publication (if available and if different from the date accessed), the title of the article, the title of the full work (if applicable) or the name of the Telnet site in italics, and the complete Telnet address, followed by a comma and directions to access the publication (if applicable). Last, give the date of visit in parentheses.

```
Dava (#472). (1995, 3 November). A deadline.
    *General (#554). Internet Public Library.
    telnet://ipl.sils.umich.edu:8888, @peek 25 on
    #554 (9 Aug. 1996).

Help. Internet public library.
    telnet://ipl.org:8888/, help (1 Dec. 1996).
```

Synchronous Communications (MOOs, MUDs, IRC, etc.) Give the name of the speaker(s), the complete date of the conversation being referenced in parentheses (if different from the date accessed), and the title of the session (if applicable). Next, list the title of the site in italics, the protocol and address (if applicable), and any directions necessary to access the work. If there is additional information such as archive addresses or file numbers (if applicable), list the word "Available," a colon, and the archival information. Last, list the date of access, enclosed in parentheses. Personal interviews do not need to be listed in the References, but do need to be included in parenthetic references in the text (see the APA *Publication Manual*).

```
Basic IRC commands. irc undernet.org, /help (13 Jan.
    1996).

Cross, J. (1996, February 27). Netoric's Tuesday
    cafe: Why use MUDs in the writing classroom?
    MediaMoo. telenet://purple-crayon.media.mit.edu:
    8888, @go Tuesday. Available: ftp://daedalus.com/
    pub/ACW/NETORIC/catalog.96a (tc 022796.log).
    (1 Mar. 1996).
```

Gopher Sites List the author's name (if applicable), the year of publication (if known and if different from the date accessed), the title of the file or paper, and the title of the complete work (if applicable). Include any print publication information (if available) followed by the protocol (i.e., gopher://) and the path necessary to access the file. List the date that the file was accessed in parentheses immediately following the path.

```
Massachusetts Higher Education Coordinating
    Council. (1994) [Online]. Using coordination
    and collaboration to address change. Available:
    gopher://gopher.mass.edu:170/00gopher_root%3A%5B_
    hecc%5D_plan.
```

Email, Listservs, and Newsgroups Give the author's name (if known), the date of the correspondence in parentheses (if known and if different from the date accessed), the subject line from the posting, and the name of the list (if known) in italics. Next, list the address of the listserv or newsgroup. Include any archival information after the address, listing the word "Available" and a colon and the protocol and address of the archive. Last, give the date accessed enclosed in parentheses. Do not include personal email in the list of References. See the APA *Publication Manual* for information on in-text citations.

Bruckman, A. S. MOOSE crossing proposal. mediamoo@media.mit.edu (20 Dec. 1994).

Heilke, J. (1996, May 3). Re: Webfolios. acw-l@ttacs. ttu.edu. Available: http://www.ttu.edu/lists/acw-l/ 9605 (31 Dec. 1996).

Laws, R. UMI thesis publication. alt.education. distance (3 Jan. 1996).

Other authors and educators have proposed similar extensions to the APA style, too. You can find URLs to these pages at

www.psychwww.com/resource/apacrib.htm

and

www.nouveaux.com/guides.htm

Another frequently-referenced set of extensions is available at

www.uvm.edu/~ncrane/estyles/apa.htm

part

2

Remember, "frequently-referenced" does not equate to "correct" or even "desirable." Check with your professor to see if your course or school has a preference for an extended APA style.

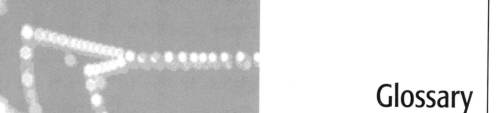

Glossary

Your Own Private Glossary

The Glossary in this book contains reference terms you'll find useful as you get started on the Internet. After a while, however, you'll find yourself running across abbreviations, acronyms, and buzzwords whose definitions will make more sense to you once you're no longer a novice (or "newbie"). That's the time to build a glossary of your own. For now, the 2DNet Webopædia gives you a place to start.

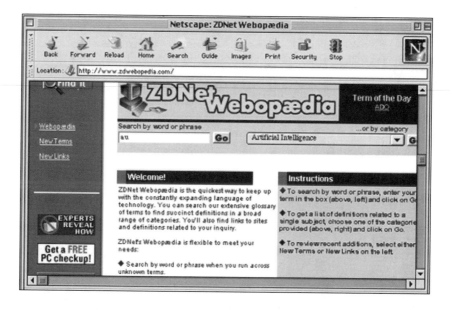

alias
A simple email address that can be used in place of a more complex one.

AVI
Audio Video Interleave. A video compression standard developed for use with Microsoft Windows. Video clips on the World Wide Web are usually available in both AVI and QuickTime formats.

bandwidth
Internet parlance for capacity to carry or transfer information such as email and Web pages.

BBS
Bulletin Board System. A dial-up computer service that allows users to post messages and download files. Some BBSs are connected to and provide access to the Internet, but many are self-contained.

browser
The computer program that lets you view the contents of Web sites.

client
A program that runs on your personal computer and supplies you with Internet services, such as getting your mail.

cyberspace
The whole universe of information that is available from computer networks. The term was coined by science fiction writer William Gibson in his novel *Neuromancer,* published in 1984.

DNS
See **domain name server.**

domain
A group of computers administered as a single unit, typically belonging to a single organization such as a university or corporation.

domain name
A name that identifies one or more computers belonging to a single domain. For example, "apple.com".

domain name server
A computer that converts domain names into the numeric addresses used on the Internet.

download
Copying a file from another computer to your computer over the Internet.

email
Electronic mail.

emoticon
A guide to the writer's feelings, represented by typed characters, such as the Smiley :-). Helps readers understand the emotions underlying a written message.

FAQ
Frequently Asked Questions

flame
A rude or derogatory message directed as a personal attack against an individual or group.

flame war
An exchange of flames (see above).

FTP
File Transfer Protocol, a method of moving files from one computer to another over the Internet.

home page
A page on the World Wide Web that acts as a starting point for information about a person or organization.

hypertext
Text that contains embedded *links* to other pages of text. Hypertext enables the reader to navigate between pages of related information by following links in the text.

LAN:
Local Area Network. A computer network that is located in a concentrated area, such as offices within a building.

link
A reference to a location on the Web that is embedded in the text of the Web page. Links are usually highlighted with a different color or underline to make them easily visible.

list server
Strictly speaking, a computer program that administers electronic mailing lists, but also used to denote such lists or discussion groups, as in "the writer's list server."

lurker
A passive reader of an Internet *newsgroup*. A lurker reads messages, but does not participate in the discussion by posting or responding to messages.

mailing list
A subject-specific automated e-mail system. Users subscribe and receive e-mail from other users about the subject of the list.

modem
A device for connecting two computers over a telephone line.

newbie
A new user of the Internet.

newsgroup
A discussion forum in which all participants can read all messages and public replies between the participants.

pages
All the text, graphics, pictures, and so forth, denoted by a single URL beginning with the identifier "http://".

plug-in
A third-party software program that will lend a web browser (Netscape, Internet Explorer, etc.) additional features.

quoted
Text in an email message or newsgroup posting that has been set off by the use of vertical bars or > characters in the left-hand margin.

search engine
A computer program that will locate Web sites or files based on specified criteria.

secure
A Web page whose contents are encrypted when sending or receiving information.

server
A computer program that moves information on request, such as a Web server that sends pages to your browser.

Smiley
See **emoticon.**

snail mail
Mail sent the old fashioned way: Write a letter, put it in an envelope, stick on a stamp, and drop it in the mailbox.

spam
Spam is to the Internet as unsolicited junk mail is to the postal system.

URL
Uniform Resource Locator: The notation for specifying addresses on the World Wide Web (e.g. http://www.abacon.com or ftp://ftp.abacon.com).

Usenet
The section of the Internet devoted to *newsgroups*.

Web browser
A program used to navigate and access information on the World Wide Web. Web browsers convert html coding into a display of pictures, sound, and words.

Web site
A collection of World Wide Web pages, usually consisting of a home page and several other linked pages.